CABELLIAN HARMONICS

By Warren A. McNeill

With an Introductory Note
by JAMES BRANCH CABELL

New York
Published by Random House
1928

Kessinger Publishing's Rare Reprints
Thousands of Scarce and Hard-to-Find Books!

PRINTED IN THE UNITED STATES OF AMERICA

CONTENTS

A Note
on Cabellian Harmonics

THIS *book I have read with extraordinary interest. For it is not always with the writings of the greatest authors, nor with exegetical comment thereupon, that our concern is most lively. Through one reason or another, some of the admittedly smaller fry may chance to appeal, in a manner less speedily to be justified than it is to be granted cordial and engaging. . . . In fact, the conceded masterpieces of literature are to most of us a bit suggestive of those officially-tended municipal and state buildings which we visit through motives distinctly disconnected from pleasure, such as paying the gas bill or inspecting dusty acres of oil paintings; whereas these smaller fry maintain private residences, howsoever time-dilapidated, in which we may hope for congenial hospitality. Not always, therefore, do we desire to spend our evenings with the very great: for example, President Coolidge is technically, at the moment I write, the greatest living American. . . .*

Well, and just so, I personally do not consider Congreve, let us say, to be a more important writer than is that other

5

William to whom the current intelligentsia no longer refer as the swan of Avon: but I, personally, do find Congreve much the more entertaining to read in and about. I find that even Sir Edmund Gosse became quite readable when he was writing about Congreve, or, for that matter, about Sir Thomas Browne. Then, too, Villon is, to me, more interesting than is Dante: Horace, as they say, "comes home" as Homer simply does not. And, in very much the same unreasoned fashion, my own personal interest in the author whom Mr. McNeill hereinafter commemorates has always been illogically deep and biassed, for reasons which are not really literary at all.

Nor does it matter that Mr. McNeill and I are not invariably at one in our interpretation of this author's text. It is a text which has diverted both of us: that seems enough, in a world not over rich in diversion. Moreover, nothing appears, to me, more strangely futile than to appraise the intentions and the "meanings" of an author in the while that he was composing any particular book. Whatsoever may be our other jurisprudent idiocies, we do not as yet consider pardoning any unlicensed felon upon the plea that his father firmly meant to beget a prohibition agent. . . . For a book, once it is printed and published, becomes individual. It is by its publication as decisively severed from its author as in parturition a child is cut off from its parent. The book "means" thereafter, perforce,—both grammatically and actually,—whatever meaning this or that reader gets out of it.

And such too, to my finding, is, by and by, the attitude of any seasoned author toward the books which he himself

6

has written, excepting only the lateliest borne. The others have gone out of his mind, into cloth bindings. Their literary ranking has been duly settled, by the Devil, known at least in our fair Southland as H. L. Mencken, and perhaps by God also, in one or another of his more thoroughly omniscient writings for THE NATION, *under the pseudonym of Clifton P. Fadiman. They have been converted into merchandise. They have become, in fine, books which their author reads very much as he reads other books.*

They are books in which he makes discoveries of, by ill luck, two kinds. But about these discoveries, if the man be fairly intelligent, as authors average, he does not say anything whatever.

—Which is, in brief, the exact reason that I do not question Mr. McNeill's interpretation of the author whom Mr. McNeill discusses. I instead end here, precisely as I began, by saying that I have read Mr. McNeill's book with extraordinary interest.

JAMES BRANCH CABELL.

Richmond-in-Virginia
April 1928

7

CHAPTER I

The Cosmic Conception

A THEORY so often suggested by James Branch Cabell that those who have read any appreciable part of the Biography must have noticed it, represents the literary man as a deity, creating a universe in which he possesses omnipotence, omniscience and the other customary attributes of divinity. The very "cream of the jest," it seems to Felix Kennaston, is that he himself may be a puppet, pulled about by a play-boy greater than himself; or perhaps he is only an imaginary figure existing in some greater mind just as the characters which Kennaston creates exist only, through the medium of his mind, in the two dimensioned world of his books.

Having shown his fondness for such a theory, one naturally would expect Mr. Cabell to exemplify it and here to point out such obvious expedients as creation of the world of Poictesme with a geography, a population and even a mythology peculiarly its own is needless. Because Poictesme is Mr. Cabell's world, and in it he is, or seems to be, omnipotent, it is useless to argue against what may to some persons appear as anachronisms, or to protest that its history and the genealogy of its inhabitants are jumbled, or that words used in the books dealing with it are not found in ordinary dictionaries, or that the themes which concern the author are not "vital." Only a citizen of this fabled world is able to judge of such matters, and to qualify as a resident, one first must take an oath of fealty to its Overlord to whom, in the guise of Horvendile, even Manuel, Redeemer of Poictesme, was required to promise allegiance. Then, having become an inhabitant, one is forced to the orthodox conclusion that whatever the God of this world has made is good.

However, while there is no novelty in pointing out Mr. Cabell's attitude of over-lordship in composing the twenty parts in the eighteen volumes of his Biography, little attention has been given heretofore to one amazing similarity between the work of this author and the handiwork of that One who fashioned the universe most of us are convinced we inhabit.

So old as to have become proverbial is the statement that the essential features of the universe are contained in a drop of water, and scientists more recently have told us that each atom is a universe in itself, containing myriads of infinitesimally small worlds in numerous tiny groups not unlike solar systems.

And, with a few qualifications, it may be stated that the essentials of the Cabellian creation, as displayed in the complete Biography, are to be observed also in single paragraphs, and almost in single sentences in the various volumes which compose it. But, to see this, one first must understand the harmonic plan according to which the Biography is built, and to do this, it is essential that one have a conception of what Mr. Cabell means when he refers to passages of "contrapuntal prose."

What apparently is the first appearance of the phrase "contrapuntal prose" in printing is found in the author's note on the Storisende edition of *Figures of Earth* where he says:

" . . . the fifteen or so experiments in contrapuntal prose were, in particular, uncharted passages from which I stayed unique in deriving pleasure where others found bewilderment and no tongue-tied irritation."

This reference served further to whet the curiosity of the writer of this paper, who already had noticed these passages with pleasurable rather than irritated bewilderment, and after attempting to chart them for himself, he began a search for similar passages in other books of the Biography.

Mr. Cabell several times came to the rescue with helpful suggestions and, as the search met with more success and passages were found not so difficult to chart, the significance of the whole idea back of this contrapuntal prose became more apparent and the Overlord of Poictesme began to appear as a maker of prose melodies.

His complete opus seemed to be the series of books which he calls the Biography—a mighty whole, symphonic in effect and treatment; each book appeared as a single movement, complete in itself, in which some one of the few recurrent themes of the Biography was developed and within the books were seen certain passages—the contrapuntal prose—which, in construction and development, seemed to sum up the plan of the entire Biography.

The term "literary craftsman," is not unfamiliar and the phrase "literary artist" likewise often is used.

11

The craftsman works skillfully, but not necessarily with artistic results; the artist, one presumes, is more successful in this regard, but his processes are likely to be wasteful.

Mr. Cabell, however, works with an artistic conception not known to the craftsman; he is too methodically careful to fall into the category which includes the artist. He has been called a literary cabinet-maker, but even the cabinet-maker throws aside many chips that will not fit into his mosaic.

The Author of the universe, however, while often prodigal, seldom appears as wasteful. New research constantly is bringing to light hidden harmonies and relationships; the stone which the builder once rejected later appears as the head of the corner and that oblivion is deep wherein are hidden his ruined models. And, as has been stated, the same plan which seems to run through the universe as a whole is discernible in many of its constituent parts.

To say that Mr. Cabell has succeeded in an attempt at similar results would be going too far but, to suggest that he has created his books watching Jahveh out of the corner of his eye, and that his glances, while often envious, must sometimes have contained a glint of the satisfaction that comes from self-recognized success, does not seem unjustified after a close examination of the now nearly completed Biography.

CHAPTER II

Symphonic Poictesme

HUGH WALPOLE first, and since then other writers, have found a unity which justifies Mr. Cabell's contention that his various books are merely parts of a single great Biography and Louis Untermyer, in his introduction to the kalki edition of *Gallantry* refers to a thesis he would like to write, saying:

"It will consider the author in his larger and less technical sense, disclosing his characters, his settings, his plots, even the entire genealogical plan of his works to be the design of a poet rather than a novelist . . . with its interrelation of figures and interweaving of themes, the Cabellian 'biography' assumes the solidarity and shapeliness of a fugue, a composition in which all the voices speak with equal precision and recurring clarity."

Mr. Untermyer's introduction was published in 1922 but his thesis, unfortunately, has not yet appeared. Rather regretfully we leave to him, or to some other one the privilege of expanding this theme in all its phases, but this study of Cabellian Harmonics would not be complete without a suggestion as to the harmony, or counterpoint in the theme of the entire Biography which may then be contrasted with the more compact presentation of a similar plan in the numerous brief contrapuntal passages.

13

Just as sonata form has its three themes—the first and second subjects and the close—so the Biography, as Mr. Cabell is making more and more clear in his notes included in the Storisende edition, is built around three subjects or themes. And these subjects are related to each other in that they are, all of them, attitudes toward life.

Beyond Life, erroneously considered by some readers to be no more than a book of literary essays, is the introductory movement of the Biography and in it are presented the major themes of the entire work.

Throughout the book the themes are expanded somewhat but, in the author's note on the Storisende edition, the reader is informed at the very outset that the Biography deals with three attitudes toward life—the chivalrous, the gallant and the poetic. Its characters are those who have, at various times, viewed life, from these several attitudes, as a testing, as a toy, and as raw material.

Beyond Life is, then, an overture not only presenting these themes, but showing also something of the principles of composition and conveying to the reader the idea that the composer is striving to attain to "the auctorial virtues of distinction and clarity, of beauty and symmetry, of tenderness and truth and urbanity."

Figures of Earth, the second book, presents more explicitly the chivalrous attitude and introduces Dom Manuel whose life, as lived by him and as perpetuated in his descendants and in the figures which he made and which Freydis endowed with life, is the chief subject matter for the Biography. Manuel himself remains always somewhat of an enigma. In *Figures of Earth* he is pictured as he appeared to those who knew him best in life while in the next book, *The Silver Stallion*, he is seen as he appeared to those same persons, and to other persons after his passing.

As to his relation to the chivalrous attitude, Mr. Cabell has said in a letter to the writer of this paper, "He (Dom Manuel), living among chivalrous conditions, appeared to some persons most brilliantly to exemplify the theory of divine vicarship, and to yet other persons seemed to be the creation of his fellows' stupidity. I take no sides. Manuel is not explained. No glimpse is ever afforded of his inner being."

Manuel's own statements, as recorded in *Figures of Earth*, are no more enlightening. His reference to the geas, or obligation, which is upon him to make some kind of a figure in the world suggests that his is the chivalrous attitude, yet he nowhere indicates that he understands the nature of this obligation and his acts are directed toward fulfilling his desires—which vanish as they are fulfilled—rather than toward performing any chivalrous service.

But, in *The Silver Stallion*, the myth about Manuel, the Redeemer, grows until he generally is recognized as the outstanding protagonist of chivalry, and those who differ from this opinion in their deeper convictions at least maintain a discreet silence in this book.

Then comes *Domnei* wherein the chivalrous attitude toward woman is revealed in the lives of Perion and Melicent, whose whole careers are dictated by the requirements of an assumption that man spends but a little time on earth and that he is here as God's vicar,

15

charged with the obligation of making any necessary sacrifice in the carrying out of his great commission.

Chivalry, the next book, deals with this attitude in a broader sense, showing in a series of stories other manifestations of the chivalrous attitude as well as that phase which is called "domnei," or woman-worship.

Having now introduced his themes and developed the first of them in such a way as to show most of its potentialities, the composer of the Biography re-introduces the theme of the poetic attitude in *The Music from Behind the Moon*, a brief book which, as will be shown later, can itself be classed only as the work of a poet. Madoc is the first of Mr. Cabell's recognized poets—although Myramon Lluagor and Manuel closely approach that classification at times—and he exemplifies the attitude of regarding life as a raw material from which something is to be made, not (as with Manuel) because there is felt an indefinite obligation to do so, nor (as with Perion) because it is an obligation owed to God, but because there is felt an inner necessity for doing so; because it is his allotted doom and because all his life yearns toward something which he cannot understand but which pushes him resistlessly in certain directions.

Having briefly re-stated his second theme, Mr. Cabell goes on, in *Jurgen*, to the third main line of his development and presents the gallant attitude exemplified in an individual, just as Perion exemplified the chivalrous attitude. Jurgen's adventures are the result of his gallant attitude—his willingness to regard life as a toy, to be played with to his heart's content. In the end, he has failed to find contentment and decides

16

that there is little joy in the playing, but the man who reaches this decision is not the gallant Jurgen, duke of Logreus, or the gallant king Jurgen of Eubonia, or the gallant Jurgen, emperor of Noumaria, or even the gallant Pope Jurgen: he is the quite common-place and middle-aged pawn-broker Jurgen.

With his three themes now presented and developed, Mr. Cabell, in his eighth book, *The Line of Love*, while establishing a connection between medieval and modern times, repeats and summarizes his treatment of the three attitudes.

"This book," he says, "is the Biography in little, dealing generally where the others handle specifically one attitude."

Thus, if one looks at the nine episodes in *The Line of Love*, it will be seen that Adhelmar in the second, and Will Sommers in the seventh are essentially chivalrous in their attitudes; Florian in the first, Falstaff in the third, Raoul de Puysange in the sixth and Falmouth in the eighth exemplify the gallant attitude, and the Sieur d'Arnaye, Francois Villon and Kit Marlowe, in the remaining episodes, all are poets.

Next comes a renewed treatment and development of the three themes. The gallant attitude, in the face of failure, is shown through the career of Florian in *The High Place* while *Gallantry*, in its series of episodes, shows the same attitude in success.

The poetic attitude gets attention in the next two books, Gerald Musgrave in *Something About Eve* finding only frustration in a life lived according to the creed of the poet while those poets who figure in the episodes of *The Certain Hour* have the same attitude and are successful in living according to their creeds.

Then come the books dealing with a more modern time. In *The Cords of Vanity* R. E. Townsend is pictured as endeavoring to live, under modern conditions, with the gallant attitude toward life, and he is no more successful than was Florian, in *The High Place*. His vain gropings and strivings are carried over into the next book, *From the Hidden Way*, of which Townsend is the nominal editor, and which contains poems written, in the main, from a gallant point of view.

Colonel Rudolph Musgrave, in *The Rivet in Grandfather's Neck*, is as much of a misfit as Townsend when the Colonel, in a modern world, tries vainly, so far as others can see, but successfully from his own standpoint, to preserve the chivalrous attitude.

Considering the plan of the Biography rather than that of the individual book, the most important character in *The Eagle's Shadow* is not Billy Woods, hero of the romantic novel, but Felix Kennaston, who exemplifies in modern times the poetic attitude. Kennaston has his own book, *The Cream of the Jest*, and while in *The Eagle's Shadow* he was a failure, in the latter book he finds success through the aid of the sigil of Scoteia and the circuit of Manuel's life is completed and returns to its starting place in Poictesme. Kennaston, like Madoc, is enamoured of the witch woman, but his method of attaining to her is different, and because of a kindly limitation placed upon him, attainment does not destroy his dream.

Straws and Prayer-Books is just outside of this completed circuit of the harmonic plan of the Biography, yet it is essential to the plan, since it deals with the author and explains why the Biography was written and *Townsend of Lichfield* also is explanatory, containing notes which serve to amplify or to explain various parts of the Biography. Thus, if the Biography is to be compared to a symphony, these two latter volumes may be likened to notes upon the composition and its author which would be printed upon concert programs.

The Jewel Merchants, inclusion of which brings the number of parts of the Biography up to twenty and so avoids a violation of the rule of the decimal system, fits easily into the general plan since its story is identical with that in "Balthasar's Daughter," one of the Episodes in *The Certain Hour*. It is like a melodious strain taken from a symphony and arranged for solo performance.

CHAPTER III

Conscious Counterpoint

LEAVING out the prologue and the epilogue, the Biography, from *Figures of Earth* to *The Cream of the Jest* swings around, thematically, and completes a circuit, as has been suggested in the preceding chapter. In this characteristic, as in others, individual volumes of the Biography epitomize the whole work.

In the first chapter of *Figures of Earth*, for example, a stranger comes upon Manuel while he is gazing into the pond of Haranton and after asking what he is staring at questions him as to a thing standing nearby. Manuel replies: "It is the figure of a man, which I have modeled and re-modeled, sir, but cannot seem to get exactly to my liking. So it is necessary that I keep laboring at it until the figure is to my thinking and my desire."

And, at the very end of the book, Grandfather Death questions Manuel as to why he is looking into a dark pool. Then Manuel sees the stranger before him and hears the question, "But what is that thing?" Again he replies: "It is the figure of a man which I have modeled and re-modeled, and cannot get exactly to my liking. So it is necessary that I keep laboring at it, until the figure is to my thinking and my desire."

One other book, *The Rivet in Grandfather's Neck*, contains equally clear verbal evidence of this circuit. Near the first of the book Colonel Musgrave meets Patricia in a garden and his impression of her then is repeated, practically word for word, at the end of the book as his final impression as he drifts off into death.

But practically all of the other books, to a greater or less extent, exhibit this characteristic of the completed circuit in idea if not in exact wording.

The Silver Stallion, for example, begins with young Jurgen's report on the disappearance of Manuel and it closes with the reflections of a much older Jurgen upon this same incident. *Domnei* opens with Perion seeing Melicent, as he thinks, for the last time, and it ends when he sees her, as he then realizes, in reality for the first time. *Jurgen* and *The High Place* each begin and end at very nearly the same point, the major incidents occuring during a period when time, as measured by other persons in the world, moves forward hardly at all, and *Something About Eve* starts with Gerald writing, as the Sylan enters his room and ends with Gerald beginning to resume his writing as the Sylan leaves. In the books consisting of separate episodes the circuit usually is made through prologues and epilogues variously titled.

Now, in line with our original contention that the plan of the Biography is compressed into single brief passages as well as being displayed in each of the books, we come more directly to what has been designated as "contrapuntal prose."

The harmony found in the Biography, in the volumes and in many passages, according to Mr. Cabell,

21

is a species of counterpoint. Fifteen passages worthy of this title were mentioned in the author's note on *Figures of Earth* but, when pressed, the author becomes less certain as to where the line should be drawn in including passages in this classification.

"The trouble," he writes, "is, of course, to determine the border line. So long as the pattern remains plainly verbal, all is plain sailing. But when the pattern is based, rather, upon the idea, then the counterpoint becomes disputable. I mean, if the reader sees it, it is there: if he misses it, the counterpoint, for all practical purposes, is not there."

That Mr. Cabell is not using "counterpoint" or "contrapuntal" in a strictly musical sense is so evident that the point need not be argued. But this leaves another question: what, then, does he imply by the term "contrapuntal prose"?

Replying to such a query he suggests the following, which he complains is "a dreadfully pompous sounding, but I believe sound definition":

"Prose counterpoint is the art of adorning one's prose with passages shaped in a pre-meditated and self-complete pattern of which the parts are correspondent, that shall harmonize with the whole and at the same time be intrinsically melodious."

Opinions may differ as to whether, under this definition, the entire Biography is written in prose counterpoint but, "if the reader sees it, it is there."

About the contrapuntal character of at least one complete book there can be less dispute, however, and many individual passages conform so closely to the definition as to leave not the slightest room for argument.

The brief book, *The Music from Behind the Moon*, because its pattern is so plainly verbal, in addition to being based upon the idea, serves as the best illustration of counterpoint in an entire volume.

The first and last brief sections of the book are a preface and a postscript, being to this book what *Beyond Life* and *Straws and Prayer-Books* are to the whole Biography and the main part of the book, which relates the tale of Madoc is in four parts, or movements of about equal length.

The first part tells how Madoc, the youngest and least prominent of the poets at the court of Netan, met a woman who "from the flesh of her body took out her red heart, and upon her heart strings she made a music,"—a strange and troubling music, so that Madoc could not put the skirling of it out of his mind. "Moreover, there was upon him a loneliness and a hungering for what he could not name." Seeking relief, Madoc obtains a quill from the wing of the Father of All Lies, and with this he writes songs approved by the most judicious at the court, but always there is upon him a feeling of discontent. He flees to another country and meets a beautiful girl who loves him, and he lives with her among a peaceful shepherd people who admire him, but Madoc is dissatisfied, "For all the while that he made this comfortable music he could hear another music, skirling: and that music derided the wholesome optimism which was in the singing and it called him, resistlessly, toward his allotted doom."

In the second part Madoc leaves the beautiful girl and seeks the company of a wise woman who loves him. She seeks to give him the drug of contentment, but he resists and stirs up so much unrest among her domestic animals who once were men that in the end she grants his request for directions to reach the waste behind the moon and the abode of the witch, Ettarre, whose skirling music he has found so troubling: "he ended his singing: and the domestic animals fell back contentedly into the incurious sloth and the fat ease of the wise woman's market-garden, out of which Madoc passed toward his allotted doom."

The third part tells how Madoc, in the waste behind the moon, found Ettarre and how he realized that it was love, not hate that had drawn him to her. He frees her from bondage by altering the prophecy of her release from captivity at the end of 725 years by changing the decimal point and making it read 7.25 years. Time runs backward some 500 years in order that the altered prophecy may be fulfilled and, mounting his hippogriffin with Ettarre, "and upon the monster's back, exulting Madoc also passed with a high heart, toward his allotted doom."

In the fourth part, Ettarre, won, proves less enticing than Ettarre unknown and, having won to her, Madoc no longer hears the skirling music she used to make. But, at last, she dies and thereafter Old Madoc hears the music once again and for him, "there stayed always yonder, always just ahead, another music, which was not wholly of this earth, and which a vagabond alone might be following after always, as was his allotted doom."

Now, as to verbal evidence to reinforce the plot which itself shows this book was "shaped in a premeditated and self-complete pattern":

The closing phrase of each of the four sections has been quoted and it will be observed that in the first, Madoc is called toward his allotted doom, in the second and third he passes toward his allotted doom and the fourth states what is his allotted doom. Such concordance of words and ideas cannot be regarded as accidental.

Only the reader who goes through the book with the idea of counterpoint in his mind can see all of the harmonies which it contains and which are not quite tangible enough to quote in brief form. But attention may be called to one example in the second part of the book where a plan is worked out quite similarly to that of the entire book. The second page of this part concludes, "and his songs which brought benevolence and vigor into the living of other persons appeared to Madoc rather silly, now that again he heard the skirling music of Ettarre."

This may be compared with the conclusion of the next page; "For always when his music soared at its most potent he heard the skirling of another music, which was all a doubtfulness and a discontent."

And then the same idea is found, in slightly altered form at the end of the next succeeding page: "it troubled Madoc that not any of the noble songs which he was making could ever wholly shut from Madoc's ears the skirling music of Ettarre."

Since quotation of the complete book is impracticable, perhaps the best way of further indicating its contrapuntal character is by citation of the preface and postscript, contained in the first and thirtieth sections, which read as follows:

I. The Text from Genesis.

To such as will to listen I plan here to tell the story of Madoc and some little part of the story of Ettarre.

Now, this is a regrettably familiar tale. It may possibly have begun with Lamech, in the Book of Genesis—who was, in any event, the first well-thought-of citizen upon known record to remark, "I have slain a young man to my hurt!" And poets tell us that since then a many poets whose bodies had survived to middle age have repeated this glum observation, although probably not ever, since then, to their co-partners alike in homicide and in married life.

Moreover, this is a regrettably inconclusive tale, without any assured ending. Nor is there any assured prophesying, either, that the next thousand years or so will remedy that defect of this tale, because the story of Ettarre is not lightly to be ended by the death of any woman's body which for the while Ettarre is wearing.

And, lastly, this is a regrettably true tale.

XXX. The Best Possible Postscript.

Such is the story of Madoc: but of the story of Ettarre this is only a very little part. For her story is not lightly to be ended (the learned declare) by the death of any woman's body which for the while Ettarre is wearing: nor is her music-making ended either (the young say), no matter to what ears time and conformity may have brought deafness.

I think we oldsters hardly need debate the affair, with so many other matters to be discussed and put in order, now that all evenings draw in. If there be any music coming from behind the moon it echoes faintlier than does the crackling of the hearth-fire, it is drowned by the piping voices of our children. We—being human,—may pause to listen now and then, half wistfully, it may be, for an unrememberable cadence which only the young hear: yet we, hearing nothing, are not wholly discontent; and common decency forbids one to disturb the home circle (as that blundering Lamech did, you will remember) by crying out, "I have slain a young man to my hurt!"

Those at all familiar with Mr. Cabell's briefer contrapuntal passages, which will be quoted hereafter, will recognize as quite characteristic the repetition, with slight variation, of the phrases "regrettably familiar tale," "regrettably inconclusive tale," and "regrettably true tale" opening the three paragraphs of the foreword, and other evidence of the careful planning of these paragraphs is seen in the close accord between the opening paragraph of the foreword and the opening paragraph of the postscript, as well as the deliberate placing of the repeated quotation from Genesis.

And, as one added bit of proof that such planning is characteristic of the Biography as a whole, another case of repetition of a paragraph may be noticed.

In *Figures of Earth*, the first book of the Biography proper, Manuel looks out of his window "over broad rolling uplands. He viewed a noble country, good to live in, rich with grain and metal, embowered with tall forests and watered by pleasant streams. Walled cities it had, and castles crowned its eminences. Very far beneath Dom Manuel the leaded roofs of fortresses glittered in the sunset, for Storisende guarded the loftiest part of all inhabited Poictesme."

Then, on page 13 of *The Cream of the Jest*, last book in which the circuit of the Biography is made, Horvendile looks out over Poictesme and the country he sees is described in identical language to that above, with the exception of three or four words, such as omission of "inhabited" in the last line.

Thus a recurrence of actual verbal sounds as well as a harmony of themes links and binds together the var-

27

ious parts of the long Biography, just as similar devices knit the chapters of individual books and the sentences of adjoining paragraphs.

CHAPTER IV

Paraphrasing the non-Existant

THE prose counterpoint of Mr. Cabell thus far has been considered in the light of his rather technical definition, but there seems a certain advantage in now introducing another, and quite informal, definition which he phrases: "Contrapuntal prose is an exact and sympathetic rendering into English of a non-existant poem." This reveals a little more clearly the attitude from which this prose is written but, as Mr. Cabell recognizes, it tends to rule out those passages which are rather faithful paraphrases of poems that do exist, in English or some other language.

The important point, however, is that the contrapuntal prose might also be classed as prose poetry, although that term too has its deficiencies: or, it might be said that the author has taken the raw stuff of verses and has chosen to use it in beautiful and orderly prose forms rather than in what technically would be accepted as poetry.

From the Hidden Way is the only book in the Biography which frankly purports to contain poetry, although poems are introduced at intervals in most of the other volumes. Most of these scattered poems are collected and re-printed in the book of verse just men-

29

tioned, but there is another book of poetry—in the broader sense—by Mr. Cabell that has yet to be collected. It consists of those, for the most part undiscovered and little known passages of "contrapuntal prose" some of which approach poetry so closely as to have regular schemes of rhyme and metre, while others are more vague in form but no less poetic in spirit.

It might be said that a collection of these passages, or at least the location and pointing out of them, would be worthwhile from the standpoint of students of prose style, and particularly those deeply interested in the manner of Mr. Cabell's writing.

But there seems a better reason for such a collation. "To write perfectly of beautiful happenings" is, one seems justified in concluding, the ambition of Mr. Cabell and that he has not altogether failed in this ambition those familiar with his books will agree. But no man can write eighteen volumes, mostly in nominal prose, and everywhere maintain an equal standard of excellency.

The real enthusiast prefers to read these volumes and discover for himself the passages of outstanding beauty; other readers are satisfied to concentrate upon one or two books in which they profess to see Cabell at his best. But, if an anthology or a "Key to Cabell" were desired, it hardly could be better chosen than from these passages of contrapuntal prose, for in them is found not only the most carefully considered work of the author, but also the very heart of the argument of the Biography as to the three attitudes toward life.

From the Hidden Way contains only the conventional verse of the Biography; its true poetry might be collected in an arrangement of the passages of contrapuntal prose.

But, where to draw the line in making such a collection, would be the difficulty. Writing in this form, at first purely conscious, no doubt, has become almost a habit with Mr. Cabell and he himself admits that he cannot say with certainty what passages are contrapuntal.

In one letter on this point he wrote: "I can give only my private opinion, in so far as possible, as a reader," and it was in this connection that he admitted the counterpoint is there only if the reader sees it.

When the writer of this paper suggested several additions to Mr. Cabell's list of passages to be included, it promptly was admitted that some of the passages mentioned had been overlooked and should be included and, at another time, he wrote: "In some places—I admit—you seem to have found more than I consciously put there. I shall profit by it, of course, and protest hereafter that it was all quite intentional."

In the following chapters only those passages are mentioned which seem, by their verbal plan as well as their poetic spirit, to conform to the definitions of contrapuntal prose already given. But the line of inclusion or exclusion is drawn purely according to the opinion of the writer. Several passages mentioned, Mr. Cabell considers as "borderline" while others which some persons might consider to have equal claim to such classification are omitted.

Considering the whole Biography, no contrapuntal passages are to be found in *From the Hidden Way*, since this book is entirely in verse. *Beyond Life* con-

31

tains no passages that get beyond the borderline, nor are there definitely planned passages to be discovered in *The Cords of Vanity, The Rivet in Grandfather's Neck* and *The Eagle's Shadow.*

All of the other books contain paragraphs which seem to merit comment and *Figures of Earth* is the logical place for the reader to look for his first introduction to this form of writing.

CHAPTER V

Figures of Earth
and Figures of Speech

WARNED by the author that there are fifteen passages of contrapuntal prose to be found in *Figures of Earth*, and having some conception of what is meant by this term, the reader probably first will have his attention attracted by the following paragraph beginning on page 19 *:

Oh, out of the void and the darkness that is peopled by Mimir's brood, from the ultimate silent fastness of the desolate deep-sea gloom, and the peace of that ageless gloom, blind Oriander came, from Mimir, to be at war with the sea and to jeer at the sea's desire. When tempests were seething and roaring from the Aesir's inverted bowl all seamen have heard his shouting and the cry that his mirth sends up: when the rim of the sea tilts up, and the world's roof wavers down, his face gleams white where distraught waves smite the Swimmer they may not tire. No eyes were allotted this Swimmer, but in blindness, with ceaseless jeers, he battles till time be done with, and the love-songs of earth be sung, and the very last dirge be sung, and the baffled and outworn sea begrudgingly own Oriander alone may mock at the might of its ire.

---

* Page references ought really to be to the Storisende, or definitive edition, but in this and following chapters it has seemed preferable (because all the volumes of the Storisende edition have not been issued and also because of the limited nature and difficulty in access to this set) to quote from the kalki edition, noting, however, instances in which a passage is revised in the later edition.

Even the fact that much of Mr. Cabell's prose has a certain rhythmic quality hardly can keep the reader from observing that this paragraph has a quite regular metre different from that of the prose by which it is surrounded.

At first one may be tempted to re-arrange the paragraph in hexameters and the first sentence will be found to fit quite well into such a scheme:

> *Oh, out of the void and the darkness that is peopled by*
> *Mimir's brood,*
> *from the ultimate silent fastness of the desolate deep-sea*
> *gloom*
> *and the peace of that ageless gloom, blind Oriander came,*
> *from Mimir, to be at war with the sea and to jeer at the*
> *sea's desire.*

But, it may further be noticed that the sentence contains certain recurring words and similar sounds. There is "darkness" rhyming with "fastness," and "gloom" is used twice, while there is assonance between this word and "brood," and "be" rhymes with "sea." It may be noticed also that the three sentences in the paragraph are of about equal length and that their ending words: "desire," "tire" and "ire" all rhyme.

Having noticed this, one might try the following arrangement of the first sentence, to make use of these rhymed endings:

> *Oh, out of the void and the darkness*
> *that is peopled by Mimir's brood,*
> *from the ultimate silent fastness*
> *of the desolate deep-sea gloom*
> *and the peace of that ageless gloom,*
> *blind Oriander came,*
> *from Mimir, to be*

34

at war with the sea
and to jeer at the sea's desire.

Such a regular and well planned verse hardly could be the result of accident, the reader will conclude, and proof that this is the correct plan, as recognized by Mr. Cabell, is found in the fact that the following two sentences contain a similar rhyme scheme and complete the poem as follows:

When tempests were seething and roaring
from the Aesir's inverted bowl
all seamen have heard his shouting
and the cry that his mirth sends up:
when the rim of the sea tilts up,
and the world's roof wavers down,
his face gleams white
where distraught waves smite
the Swimmer they may not tire.

No eyes were allotted this Swimmer,
but in blindness, with ceaseless jeers,
he battles till time be done with,
and the love-songs of earth be sung,
and the very last dirge be sung,
and the baffled and outworn sea
begrudgingly own
Oriander alone
may mock at the might of its ire.

Here it will seem that the definition of contrapuntal prose as "the exact and sympathetic rendering into English of a non-existant poem" is a little strained because, the poem no longer is non-existant except in typographical form. Yet, in the book, it looks like prose and many persons have read it through without

35

suspecting the possibility of there being another form in which it might have been printed.

Going on through the book, the discerning reader may next stop on page 26 when he reads Myramon Lluagor's speech to Manuel which begins, "Love, as I think, is an instant's fusing of shadow and substance." Once again, the rhythm makes an impression and, having read through the passage and on to the next page, a clue to its proper form is found in Manuel's remark, "I never quite understood hexameters."

Following so broad a hint, there is little difficulty in arranging the complete passage in the following form:

Love, as I think, is an instant's fusing of shadow and
substance.
They that aspire to possess love utterly, fall into folly.
This is forbidden: you cannot. The lover, beholding that
fusing
move as a golden-hued goddess, accessible, kindly and
priceless,
wooes and ill-fatedly wins all the substance. The golden-
hued shadow
dims in the dawn of his married life, dulled with content
and the shadow
vanishes. So there remains for the puzzled husband's em-
bracing,
flesh which is fair and dear, no doubt, yet is flesh such as
his; and
talking and talking and talking; and kisses in all ways
desirable.
Love, of a sort too remains, but hardly the love that was
yesterday's.

This is the cry of all husbands that now are or may be
hereafter,—
"What has become of the girl that I married? and how
shall I rightly

deal with this woman whom somehow time has involved
in my doings?
Love, of a sort, now I have for her, but not the love that
was yesterday's.

Yes, he is wiser that shelters his longing from any such
surfeit.
Yes, he is wiser that knows the shadow makes lovely the
substance,
wisely regarding the ways of that irresponsible shadow
which, if you grasp at it, flees, and, when you avoid it,
will follow,
gilding all life with its glory and keeping always one
woman
young and most fair and most wise and unwon; and
keeping you always
never contented, but armed with a self respect that no
husband
manages quite to retain in the face of being contented.
No, for love is an instant's fusing of shadow and substance,
fused for an instant only, whereafter the lover may harvest
pleasure from either alone, but hardly from these two
united.

The hexameters in the above passage are indisputable and as for counterpoint, it may be observed that, from a purely verbal standpoint, there is the close accord between the opening and the closing (once again, the complete circuit is made) of the passage and the echo-like endings of the first and second sections. But here, as in other passages, there is a species of counterpoint in the entire passage that cannot very definitely be explained or pointed out; it must be, and can be, felt rather than shown.

Turning, then, to page 60, the reader finds another passage which possesses unquestionable rhythm and a kind of rhyme is easily discernible in repetition of the same words or of the same vowel, rather than consonant sounds.

Any one familiar with the metre of Swinburne's "Triumph of Time," will have no difficulty in arranging this passage according to the plan of that poem, as is shown below. Manuel is the speaker:

> *I ride to encounter what life has in store for me,*
> *who am made certain of this at least,*
> *that all high harvest which life withholds for me*
> *springs from a seed which I sow—and reap.*
> *For my geas is potent, and, late or soon,*
> *I serve my geas, and take my doom*
> *as the pay well earned that is given as pay to me,*
> *for the figure I make in this world of men.*
>
> *This figure, foreseen and yet hidden away from me,*
> *glimpsed from afar in the light of a dream,—*
> *will I love it, once made, or will loathing awake in me*
> *after its visage is plainlier seen?*
> *No matter: as fate says so say I,*
> *who serve my geas and gain in time*
> *such payment, at worst, as is honestly due to me,*
> *for the figure I make in this world of men.*
>
> *To its shaping I consecrate youth that is strong in me,*
> *ardently yielding youth's last least gift,*
> *who know that all grace which the gods have allotted me*
> *avails me in naught if it fails me in this.*
> *For all that a man has, that must I bring*
> *to the image I shape, that my making may live*
> *when time unmakes me and death dissevers me*
> *from the figure I make in this world of men.*

So far all the passages quoted have seemed to belie the statement that they are prose renderings of unwritten poems, since they appear to be poems in themselves, but on page 110 is found a truer example of these "experiments" in prose counterpoint. The passage begins:

I cry the elegy of such notions as are possible to boys alone. "Surely," I said, "the informing and all-perfect soul shines through and is revealed in this beautiful body!" So my worship began for you, whose violet eyes retain at all times their chill brittle shining, and do not soften, but have been to me always as those eyes which, they say, the goddess turns toward poor ruined lovers who cry the elegy of hope and contentment, with lips burned bloodless by the searing of passions which she, immortal, may neither feel nor comprehend. Even so do you, dear Alianora, who are not divine, look toward me, quite unmoved by anything except incurious wonder, the while that I cry my elegy.

It seems improbable that Mr. Cabell had any verse form in mind when he wrote this and the two succeeding paragraphs, but that they were carefully planned according to his idea of prose counterpoint seems equally evident. Not because he intended any such arrangement, but for the sake of emphasizing the recurrent use of words and sounds to give the passage its poetic quality, the following division into lines is suggested,— and it will be noticed that the three paragraphs fall into forty-nine lines which end in a total of only nine sounds, and the repetition of these sounds, while not regular, is such as to hint at a conscious planning:

I cry the elegy
of such notions as are possible to boys alone. "Surely,"
I said, "the informing and all-perfect soul shines through
and is revealed in this beautiful body."
So my worship began for you,
whose violet eyes retain at all times their brilliant shining,

39

and do not soften, but have been to me
always as those eyes which, they say, a goddess
turns toward ruined lovers who cry the elegy
of hope and contentment, with lips burned bloodless
by the searing of passions which she,
immortal, may neither feel nor comprehend. Even so
                                        do you,
dear Alianora, who are not divine, look toward me,
quite unmoved by anything except incurious wonder,
the while that I cry my elegy.

I, for love,
and for the glamour of bright beguiling dreams that hover
and delude and allure all lovers, could never
until today behold clearly what person I was pestering
with my notions. I, being
blind, could not perceive your blindness which blindly
strove to understand me,
and which hungered for understanding,
as I for love.
Thus our kisses veiled, at most, the foiled endeavor-
ings of flesh that willingly would enter
into the soul's high places, but is
not able. Now, the game being over, what is
the issue and end of it time must attest. At least we
should each sorrow a little for what we
have lost in this gaming—
you for a lover,
and I for love.

No, but it is not love
which lies here expiring, now we part friendlily
at the deathbed of that emotion
which yesterday we shared. This emotion
also was not divine; and so might not outlive the gainless
months wherein, like one
fishing for pearls in a mill-pond I have toiled to

40

evoke from your heart more than Heaven
placed in this heart, wherein lies no love.
Now the crying is stilled that was the crying of loneliness
to its unfound mate: already
dust is gathering light and grey upon
the unmoving lips. Therefore let us bury
our dead, and having placed the body in the tomb, let us
*   honestly*
inscribe above the fragile, flower-like perished emotion,
"Here lieth lust, not love."

Especially noticeable in the above passage is the repetition, with slight variations, of a phrase at the beginning, the middle and the end of each paragraph. Thus, in each of these paragraphs there is made a circuit of thought and of sound not unlike those completed in the various volumes and in the biography as a whole.

Then, on page 125 is found a passage consisting of three paragraphs each beginning "Freydis am I, the dread high Queen of Audela." In the Storisende edition (page 102) this same passage appears but the opening sentence, in each instance, reads, "The land of Audela is my kingdom." The revised form is chosen for quotation.

Here the counterpoint is too vague in verbal plan to be shown by a re-arrangement of the lines, but that it exists is indicated by the recurring words that are italicized below:

The land of Audela is my *kingdom*. But you embraced my penalties, and made a human woman of me. So do I tread with wraiths, for my lost realm alone is real. Here all is but a restless contention of *shadows* that pass presently; here all that is visible and all the *colors* known to men are *shadows*, dimming the true

41

colors, and time and death, the darkest *shadows* known to men, delude you with false seemings: for all such things as men hold incontestable, because they are apparent to *sight and sense*, are a weariful drifting of fogs that *veil* the world which is no longer mine. So in this twilit world of yours do we of Audela appear to be but *men and women*.

The land of Audela is my *kingdom* where I am Queen of all that lies behind this *veil* of human *sight and sense*. This *veil* may not be lifted, but very often the *veil* is pierced, and noting the broken places, men call it fire. Through these torn places men may *glimpse* the world that is real: and this *glimpse* dazzles their dimmed eyes and weakling forces, and this *glimpse* mocks at their lean might. Through these rent places, when the opening is made large enough, a few men here and there, not quite so witless as their fellows, know how to summon us of Audela when for an hour the moon is void and powerless: we come for an old reason: and we come as *men and women*.

The land of Audela is my *kingdom* and very often, just *for the sport's sake*, do I and my servitors go secretly among you. As human beings we blunder about in your darkened *shadow* world, bound by the laws of *sight and sense*, but keeping always in our hearts the *secrets* of Audela and the *secret* of our manner of returning thither. Sometimes, too, *for the sport's sake*, we imprison in earthen figures a spark of the true *life* of Audela: and then you little persons, that have no authentic *life*, but only the flickering of a vexed *shadow* to sustain you in brief fretfulness, say it is very pretty; and you negligently applaud us as the most trivial of *men and women*.

Here again is seen the completed circuit and (perhaps it is a coincidence) if one should take the trouble to set down the italicized words in the above paragraphs in the order in which they first occur, omitting only "for the sport's sake," and adding only articles and connectives, the theme of the passage is not-inadequately stated in the following sentence:

42

The *kingdom* of *shadows* and *colors*, of *sight and sense veils* from *men and women* a *glimpse* of the *secrets* of *life*.

Still following the plan of re-arranging the contrapuntal prose in various suggestive patterns, not necessarily because Mr. Cabell intended them to be so arranged, but because such a device may help the reader to glimpse the elements which give them their peculiar harmonic quality, the passage found beginning on page 129 may be considered as a responsive reading.

Manuel is the speaker throughout in the book, but if the sentences of each paragraph are separated and are conceived of as being read alternately by first and second voices with a chorus coming in on the last sentence of each paragraph, which is, indeed, the refrain, the counterpoint becomes evident, as may be seen below:

I.

There is much loss in the world, where men war ceaselessly with sorrow, and time like a strong thief strips all men of all they prize.

Yet when the emperor is beaten in battle and his broad lands are lost, he, shrugging, says, "In the next battle I may conquer."

And when the bearded merchant's ship is lost at sea, he says, "The next voyage, belike, will be prosperous."

Even when the life of an old beggar departs from him in a ditch, he says, "I trust tomorrow to be a glad young seraph in paradise."

Thus hope serves as a cordial to every hurt: but for him who has beheld the loveliness of Freydis there is no hope at all.

II.

For in comparison with that alien clear beauty there is no beauty in this world.

He that has beheld the loveliness of Freydis must go henceforward as a hungry person, because of troubling memories: and his fellows deride him enviously.

All the world is fretted by his folly, knowing that his faith in the world's might is no longer firm-set, and that he aspires to what is beyond the world's giving.

In his heart he belittles the strong stupid lords of earth; and they, being strong, plan vengeance, the while that in a corner he is making images to commemorate what is lost:

And so for him who has beheld the loveliness of Freydis there is no hope at all.

III.

He that has willed to look upon Queen Freydis does not dread to consort with serpents nor with swine;

he faces the mirror wherein a man beholds himself without self-deceiving;

he views the blood that drips from his soiled hands, and knows that this, too, was needed:

yet these endurings purchase but one hour.

The hour passes, and therewith passes also Freydis, the high Queen.

Only the memory of her hour remains, like a cruel gadfly for which the crazed beholder of Queen Freydis must build a lodging in his images, madly endeavoring to commingle memories with wet mud:

and so for him who has beheld the loveliness of Freydis there is no hope at all.

Turning, then, to page 152, the reader finds one of the most interesting experiments in this book. It is, as Freydis explains to Manuel, "an unfinished incantation in that it is a bit of unfinished magic for which the proper words have not yet been found; but between now and a while they will be stumbled on, and then this rune will live perpetually, surviving those rhymes that are infected with thought and intelligent meanings such as are repugnant to human nature."

44

The passage further is designated as "the unfinished Rune of the Blackbirds," and the first paragraph can, without great difficulty if one will but notice the rhymed sounds, be re-arranged in the following form:

Crammed and squeezed, so entombed (on some wager,
I hazard), in spite of scared squawkings and mutter,
after the fashion that lean-faced Rajah!
dealt with trapped heroes, once, in Calcutta.
Dared you break the crust and bullyrag 'em—hot,
fierce and angry, what wide beaks buzz
plain Saxon as ever spoke Witengamot!
Yet, singing, they sing as no white bird does
(where none rears phoenix) as near perfection
as nature gets, or, if scowls bar platitude,
notes for which there is no rejection,
in banks whose coinage—oh, neat!—is gratitude.

One suspects that here Mr. Cabell is indulging a rare inclination to become didactic and present an object lesson on the value of the auctorial virtue of clarity because, this confusing verse is, after all, when the proper words are found for the paraphrase, rather easily comparable, almost line for line with the quite familiar:

"Sing a song of six-pence,
A pocket full of rye,
Four and twenty blackbirds
Baked in a pie.
When the pie was opened,
All the birds began to sing;
Wasn't that a pretty dish
To set before the king?"

Then, if one has in mind the next verse:

"The king was in the counting house,
Counting out his money;

45

The queen was in the parlor,
Eating bread and honey.
The maid was in the garden
Hanging out the clothes:
Along came a blackbird,
And nipped off her nose."

it becomes still easier to re-arrange the next of Mr. Cabell's paragraphs in verse form and to see it as a grandiose paraphrase:

But far from their choiring the high king sat,
in a gold-faced vest and a gold-laced hat,
counting heaped monies, and dreaming of more
francs and sequins and Louis d'or.
Meanwhile the Queen on that fateful night,
though vowing her lack of all appetite,
was still at table, where, rumour said,
she was smearing her seventh slice of bread
(thus each turgescible rumour thrives
at court) with gold from the royal hives.
Through slumberous parc, under arching trees,
to her labors went singing the maid Denise.

So far the parallelism has been plain enough, but in the next paragraph, an element is introduced that at first may be puzzling to the reader:

And she sang of how subtle and bitter and bright was a
beast brought forth,
that was clad in the splendor and light of the cold fair
ends of the north,
like a fleshly blossom more white than augmenting tem-
pests that go,
with thunder for weapon, to ravage the strait waste fast-
ness of snow.
She sang how that all men on earth said, whether its mis-
tress at morn
went forth or waited till night,—whether she strive through
the foam

46

and wreckage of shallow and firth, or couched in glad
fields of corn,
or fled from all human delight,—that thither it likewise
would roam.

This may be regarded as the song of the maid, just before she is attacked by the blackbird, but it takes a deal of elimination of grand language to bring out the fact that the "beast" described in the first half of the paragraph above is a lamb, whose "fleece was white as snow," and the recitation of the adventures its mistress might have had obscures the concluding statement to the effect that "Everywhere that Mary went, the lamb was sure to go"!

In the fourth paragraph, which falls into blank verse, the author returns to the blackbird rhyme and the incident of the nipped-off nose, preserving still the heroic style:

Thus sang Denise, what while the siccant sheets
and coverlets that pillowed kingly dreams,
with curious undergarbs of royalty,
she neatly ranged: and dreamed not of that doom
which waited, yet unborn, to strike men dumb
with perfect awe. As when the seventh wave
poises and sunlight cleaves it through and through
with gold, as though to gild oncoming death
for him that sees foredoomed—and, gasping, sees
death high and splendid!—while the tall wave bears
down, and its shattering makes an end of him:
thus poised the sable bird while one might count
one, two, and three, and four, and five, and six,
but hardly seven—.

Continuing through the book, the next five contrapuntal passages to be noticed are less striking in verbal plan than those already noticed. The characteristic by

47

which they may be recognized is a repeated sentence or clause at the beginning, or the end of successive paragraphs, usually from three to five in number. When read, these paragraphs have an harmonic quality, but the exact words and phrases which produce this are difficult to locate.

On page 157, for example, Manuel begins, "But I cannot put aside the thought that these men ought to be my fellows and my intimates."

The familiar circuit is made when the paragraph ends, "And that thought also is a grief." The two following paragraphs are of about similar length and construction, each beginning, "But I cannot put aside the thought," and ending, "that thought also is a grief."

On page 163 begins a passage of five paragraphs, each ending in the phrase "all that is worthiest in the old time," and describing the treasure vaults of Death as the ultimate goal of all that is most valuable and, hence, showing the improbability of anyone being able to bribe this so opulent Death. And, beginning on page 193 is a discourse of Misery which begins, "Take no fear for not seeing me again, now that you are about once more to become human. Certainly, Niafer, I must leave you for a little while, but certainly I shall return."

Was it with conscious irony, one wonders, that this passage containing the glum re-assurance of the eternal presence of Misery was made closely to parallel the parting re-assurance of Jesus to his apostles? The passage, at any event, is distinguishable in the book by the repeated line at the end of each paragraph, "And I, whom some call Beda, and others call Kruchina, shall be monstrously amused by this."

48

It is the Stork who speaks in the passage beginning on page 230, "I bring the children, stainless and dear and helpless," and three paragraphs begin in the same manner. Then, on page 255 Manuel says: "Under your dear bewitchments, Sesphra, I confess that through love men win to sick disgust and self-despising, and for that reason I will not love any more." This and the three succeeding paragraphs conclude with the phrase "dear bewitchments," used in varying connections.

Coming, then, to page 284, the reader finds Myramon Lluagor as the speaker, and once again the wizard falls into hexameters, as is seen by the following rearrangement of the three paragraphs of his address to the ten redeemers he has summoned to win Poictesme for Manuel:

*You whom I made for man's worship when earth was
      younger and fairer,
hearken, and learn why I breathe new life into husks
      from my scrap-heaps!
Gods of old days, discrowned, disjected, and treated as
      rubbish,
hark to the latest way of the folk whose fathers you succored!
They have discarded you utterly. Such as remember de-
      ride you, saying:*

*"The brawling old lords that our grandfathers honored
      have perished,
if they indeed were ever more than some curious notions
bred of our grandfathers' questing, that looked to find
      God in each rainstorm
coming to nourish their barley, and God in the heat-
      bringing sun, and
God in the earth which gave life. Even so was each hour of
      their living*

touched with odd notions of God and with lunacies as to
                                        God's kindness.
We are more sensible people, for we understand all about
                                        the
freaks of the wind and the weather, and find them in no
                                        way astounding.
As for whatever gods may exist, they are civil, in that they
let us alone in our life-time; and so we return their polite-
                                        ness,
knowing that what we are doing on earth is important
                                        enough to
need undivided attention."

                    Such are the folk that deride you,
such are the folk that ignore the gods whom Miramon
                                        fashioned,
such are the folk whom today I permit you freely to
                                        deal with
after the manner of gods. Do you now make the most of
                                        your chance, and
devastate all Poictesme in time for an earlyish supper!

And next, on page 295, one finds one of the most
interestingly planned passages in the book. Here prose
and verse skillfully are blended. There is a definite
rhyme scheme and metrical lines, but arrangement of
these in verse form is made impossible by their spac-
ing between clauses of prose.

If, in the following quotation, italicized words are
noticed, it will be seen that each of the nine sentences
in the three paragraphs opens with a line containing
six iambic feet at the end of which is a word rhyming
with the concluding word in the sentence: and this
concluding word is preceded by a line containing five
iambic feet. Thus, in the first sentence, "Yes, but the
long low sobbing of the violin . . . speaks of what was

and of what might have been," is the verse part, intervening clauses being prose:

Yes, but the long low sobbing of the *violin*, troubling as the vague thoughts begotten by that season wherein summer is not yet perished from the earth, but lingers wanly in the tattered shrines of summer, speaks of what was and of what might have *been*. A blind desire, the same which on warm moonlight *nights* was used to shake like fever in the veins of a boy whom I remember, is futilely plaguing a gray fellow with the gray wraiths of innumerable old griefs and with small stinging memories of long-dead *delights*. Such thirsting breeds no good for staid and aging *men*, but my lips are athirst for lips whose loveliness no longer exists in flesh, and I thirst for a dead time and its dead fervors to be reviving, so that young Manuel may love *again*.

To-night now surely somewhere, while this music *sets* uncertain and probing fingers to healed wounds, an aging woman, in everything a stranger to me, is troubled just thus futilely, and she too remembers what she half *forgets*. "We that of old were one, and shuddered heart to *heart*, with our young lips and our souls too made indivisible,"—thus she is thinking, as I think,—"has life dealt candidly in leaving us to potter with half measures and to make nothing of severed lives that shrivel far *apart?*" Yes, she to-night is sad as I, it well may *be;* but I cannot rest certain of this because there is in young love a glory so bedazzling as to prevent the lover from seeing clearly his co-worshipper, and therefore in that dear time when we served love together I learned no more of her than she of *me*.

Of all my failures this is bitterest to *bear*, that out of so much grieving and aspiring I have gained no assured knowledge of the woman herself, but must perforce become lachrymose over such perished tinsels as her quivering red lips and shining *hair!* Of youth and love is there no more, then, to be *won* than virginal breasts and a small white belly yielded to the will of the lover, and brief drunkenness, and afterward such puzzled yearning as now dies into acquiescence, very much as the long low sobbing of that violin yonder dies into stillness now that the song is *done?*

And here, in addition to the internal planning, there is made the usual circuit from beginning to end, as evidenced in the repetition of "the long low sobbing of the violin."

The fifteenth, and last, contrapuntal passage in this book seems to begin on page 336 and is more complicated in form than the preceding ones. Indeed, its plan approximates more closely that of the Biography as a whole, for here too there are three "refrains," serving as themes and the entire passage consists of repetition and development of these, with certain intervening paragraphs that might be regarded as "rests" or interludes.

The first and second subjects are found, respectively, in the opening and closing phrases, which are italicized, of the following paragraph with which the passage opens:

"Weep, weep for Suskind!" then said Lubrican, wailing feebly in the gray and April-scented dusk: "for it was she alone who knew the secret of preserving that dissatisfaction which is divine where all else *falls away into the acquiescence of beasts.*

The third subject, or "close" is the concluding phrase of the next paragraph:

"Why, yes, but happiness is not the true desire of man," says Manuel. "I know for I have had both happiness and unhappiness, *and neither contented me.*"

The next two paragraphs re-introduce and develop these same themes:

"Weep, weep for Suskind!" then cried the soft and delicate voice of Hinzelmann: "for it was she that would have loved you, Manuel, with that love of which youth dreams, and which exists nowhere upon your side of the window, where all kissed women

turn to stupid figures of warm earth, and all love *falls away* with age *into the acquiescence of beasts.*"

"Oh, it is very true," said Manuel, "that all my life henceforward will be a wearying business because of long desires for Suskind's love and Suskind's lips and the grave beauty of her youth, and for all the high hearted dissatisfactions of youth. But the Alf charm is lifted from the head of my child, and Melicent will live as Niafer lives, and it will be better for all of us, and *I am content.*"

It will be noticed that, as might be the case in musical composition, the third theme has here been reversed: in the next paragraph the first theme is handled almost as in an anthem:

And now from below came many voices wailing confusedly. "We *weep for Suskind.* Suskind is slain with the one weapon that might slay her: and all we *weep for Suskind,* who was the fairest and the wisest and the most unreasonable of queens. Let all the hidden children *weep for Suskind,* whose heart was the life of April, and who plotted courageously against the orderings of unimaginative gods, and who has been butchered to preserve the hair of a quite ordinary child."

Then, serving as an interlude, comes a paragraph dealing with changes that have taken place in Manuel and in which the themes are not repeated. Afterward one reads three paragraphs in which the first theme is elaborated and the other two themes are re-introduced:

"We weep, and with long weeping raise the dirge for Suskind—!"
"But I, who do not weep,—I *raise the dirge* for Manuel. For I must henceforward be reasonable in all things, and I shall never be quite *discontented* any more: and I must feed and sleep as the beasts do, and it may be that I shall even fall to thinking complacently about my death and glorious resurrection. Yes, yes, all this is certain, and I may not ever go a-travelling everywhither to see the ends of this world and judge them: and the desire to do so no longer moves in me, for there is a cloud about my goings,

53

and there is a whispering that follows me, and I too *fall away into the acquiescence of beasts.* Meanwhile no hair of the child's head has been injured, and *I am content.*"

"Let all the hidden children, and all else that lives except the tall gray son of Oriander, whose blood is harsh sea-water, *weep for Suskind!* Suskind is dead, that was unstained by human sin and unredeemed by Christ's dear blood, and youth has perished from the world. Oh, let us weep, for all the world grows chill and gray as Oriander's son."

And in the next paragraph, Manuel concludes the passage with the sentence:

"But I am certain that no hair of the child's head has been injured, and I am certain that *I am content.*"

Of all the passages designated as contrapuntal prose, the one just described is, perhaps, constructed most closely according to principles of counterpoint as they apply in music. Yet, at the same time, it conforms also to Mr. Cabell's definitions of this form of writing.

54

CHAPTER VI

Vagrancies of a Verse-Maker

VOLUMES which go to make up the Biography vary in the frequency with which passages of contrapuntal prose occur in them. As compared with the fifteen passages in *Figures of Earth*, only one, or possibly two passages are to be found in *The Silver Stallion*, although this book contains other paragraphs which are on the borderline.

On page 18 one reads, "Then Anavelt of Fomor made a lament for the passing of that noble order whose ranks were broken at last, and for Dom Manuel also Anavelt raised a lament, praising Manuel for his hardihood and his cunning and his terribleness in battle."

The lament which follows approaches the contrapuntal form, being in three paragraphs beginning, severally, "Manuel was hardy," "Manuel was cunning," and "Manuel was terrible."

An example of the borderline passages in this book is that beginning on page 257. Balthis, just having discovered that her husband Ninzian is a devil, speaks and the first paragraph of her rebuke ends: "and I leave it to your conscience if, after the way I have worked and slaved for you, you had the right to play this wrong and treachery upon me."

The next paragraph begins: "For it is a great wrong and treachery which you have played upon me," and the third paragraph ends, "on account of the great wrong and treachery which you have played upon me."

Leaving this book, however, and going to the next in the series, *Domnei* is found to contain a number of especially interesting experiments some of which do not conform to Mr. Cabell's briefer definition of contrapuntal prose because they are paraphrases of existing poems.

On page 78 of this book one encounters a passage which is changed somewhat in the Storisende edition (where it appears on page 74) to read as follows:

I love you, Melicent, and you do not love me. Do not be offended because my speech is harsh, for even though I know my candor is distasteful I must speak the truth. You have been obdurate too long, denying Kypris what is due to her. I think that your brain is giddy because of too much exulting in the magnificence of your body and in the number of men who have desired it to their own hurt. I concede your beauty, yet what will it matter a hundred years from now?

I admit that my refrain is old. But it will presently take on a more poignant meaning, because a hundred years from now you—even you, O most detestable one, and all that loveliness which causes me to estimate life as a light matter in comparison with your love, will be only a bone or two. Your lustrous eyes, which are now more beautiful than it is possible to express, will be unsavory holes and a worm will crawl through them; and what will it matter a hundred years from now?

A hundred years from now no man will find Melicent to be more admirable than Demetrios. One skull is like another, and is as lightly crushed by the busy plow of the farmer. You will be as ugly as I, and nobody will be thinking of your eyes and hair. Hail, rain and dew will drench us both impartially when I lie at your side, as I intend to do, for a hundred years and yet another hundred years. You need not frown, for what will it matter a hundred years from now?

Melicent, I offer love and a life that derides the folly of all other manners of living; and whether you heed me or deny me, what will it matter a hundred years from now?

Domnei, which first was published under the title, "The Soul of Melicent," purports to be translated from an old work by Nicolas de Caen and so, if one turns to page 71 of *From the Hidden Way*, it is not surprising to find a note "After Nicolas de Caen" preceding the following poem entitled, "Comfort for Centenarians."

Marvel not if my words are bold;
Though the sound be rude, yet the sense is true;
Too long you have flouted a tale oft-told
By the stammering tongues of men that woo,
And woo you vainly. Your brain is askew
For pride in your body's magnificence,
And its color and curving so fair to view;—
And what will it matter a hundred years hence?

My burden, I grant you, is blunt and old:
Yet time will sharpen its sting when you—
Even you yourself!—and the things you hold
At so dear a price are a bone or two;
And those wonderful eyes, whose heaven-like blue
Is the crown of your beauty's excellence,
Are unsavory holes that a worm crawls through;—
And what will it matter a hundred years hence?

Encrusted and tainted with churchyard mould,
Your dear perfections must lie perdue;
Take on such favor as few behold
With liking, and certainly none pursue.

And your beauty be reft of all revenue,
And suffer the blind worm's insolence,
Who recks not at all of height, hair and hue,—
And what will it matter a hundred years hence?

Ettarre, I proffer my love anew,
And life, with a jest at the world's expense;
And if for your favor I vainly sue—
Why what will it matter a hundred years hence?

And if further evidence is desired to show that this parallelism of prose and verse is not accidental, it may be found in the "Apologia Auctoris" for *From the Hidden Way* where it is stated that Nicolas de Caen "has, at any event, afforded the late Mr. Howard Pyle the subject matter for some striking paintings." Here it is recalled that "The Soul of Melicent" was illustrated in color by Mr. Pyle.

Another variation of the prose counterpoint is found on page 90 of *Domnei* in a passage beginning with the two following paragraphs:

Perion said:

"It is the memory of a fair and noble lady, Messire Demetrios, that causes me to heave a sigh from my inmost heart. I cannot forget that loveliness which had no parallel. Pardieu, her eyes were amethysts, her lips were red as the berries of a holly-tree. Her hair blazed in the light, bright as the sunflower glows; her skin was whiter than milk; the down of a fledgling bird was not more grateful to the touch than were her hands. There was never any person more delightful to gaze upon, and whosoever beheld her forthwith desired to render love and service to Dame Melicent."

Demetrios said:

"She is still a brightly-colored creature, moves gracefully, has a sweet, drowsy voice, and is as soft to the touch as rabbit's fur. Therefore, it is imperative that one of us must cut the other's throat. The deduction is perfectly logical. Yet I do not know that my love for her is any greater than my hatred. I rage against her patient tolerance of me, and I am often tempted to disfigure, mutilate, even to destroy this colorful stupid woman, who makes me woefully ridiculous in my own eyes. I shall be happier when death has taken the woman who ventures to deal in this fashion with Demetrios."

In two more paragraphs of approximately the same length as these, and each ending, "love and service to Dame Melicent," Perion speaks, being followed in each case by a paragraph in which Demetrios speaks and concludes, "ventures to deal in this fashion with Demetrios."

Then come the following concluding paragraphs, so that the complete passage has very much the form of a double poem of the type already quoted under the title, "Comfort for Centenarians."

"Demetrios, already your antics are laughable, for you pass blindly by the revelation of heaven's splendour in heaven's masterwork; you ignore the miracle; and so do you find only the stings of the flesh where I find joy in rendering love and service to Dame Melicent."

"Perion, it is you that play the fool, in not recognizing that heaven is inaccessible and doubtful. But clearer eyes perceive the not at all doubtful dullness of wit, and the gratifying accessibility of every woman when properly handled,—yes, even of her who dares to deal in this fashion with Demetrios."

In the next paragraph it is said of Perion and Demetrios that "they would sit together . . . and speak against each other in the manner of a Tenson."

Leaving *Domnei*, for the moment, and turning to *Chivalry*, the next book in the Biography, omitting *The Music from Behind the Moon*, which already has

59

been considered, one may be attracted by the title of one episode called: "The Story of the Tenson." Looking in this for such prose counterpoint as that just quoted from *Domnei*, the reader will find, beginning on page 56, Miguel and the Prince singing against each other.

Miguel begins:

Passeth a little while, and Irus the beggar and Menephtah the high king are at sorry unison, and Guenevere is a skull. Multitudinously we tread toward oblivion, as ants hasten toward sugar, and presently Time cometh with his broom. Multitudinously we tread a dusty road toward oblivion; but yonder the sun shines upon a grass-plot, converting it into an emerald; and I am aweary of the trodden path.

The three paragraphs that follow are similar in structure and the last of them is shorter and in the form of an envoi addressed to the Prince. Each ends "aweary of the trodden path," and then the Prince begins:

I was in a path, and I trod toward the citadel of the land's seigneur, and on either side were pleasant and forbidden meadows, having various names. And one treading with me babbled of brooding mountains and of low-lying and adjacent clouds; of the west wind and the budding fruit trees. He debated the significance of these things, and he went astray to gather violets, while I walked in the trodden path.

This too is followed by three paragraphs, the last of them shorter and addressed to Miguel and each ending, "I walked in the trodden path."

And in this book the passages here referred to are distinguished from surrounding prose by being printed in italics.

Returning to *Domnei*, on page 134 is found a conversation between Perion and Melusine not quite dis-

60

tinctive enough in form to be classed definitely as contrapuntal, yet strongly reminiscent of a poem in *From the Hidden Way*.

Melusine says: "For us the spring is only a dotard sorcerer who has forgotten the spells of yesterday. And I think that it is pitiable, although I would not have it otherwise."

And on page 94 of the book of verse a poem entitled, "The Dotard Conjurer," contains the following:

> *Here the old magic works not any more;*
> *And spring, a dotard conjurer, forgets*
> *The runes and sorceries of yesterday,*
> *And may at best evoke but tenuous visions,—*
> *Faint hearted dreams that people the turbid past*
> *With half-seen faces and derisive laughter;—*
> *And there is nothing hidden in the woods*
> *Save birds, and trees, and flowers, and ravenous gnats,*
> *And under all, dead and decaying leaves.*

Two more examples of the single "Tenson" form of the prose counterpoint are found in *Domnei*. On page 150 Melicent says:

It is not unlikely that the Perion men know today has forgotten me and the service which I joyed to render Perion. Let him who would understand the mystery of the Crucifixion first become a lover! I pray for the old sake's sake that Perion and his lady may taste of every prosperity. Indeed, I do not envy her. Rather I pity her, because last night I wandered through a certain forest hand-in-hand with a young Perion, whose excellencies she will never know as I know them in our own woods.

The next two paragraphs end, "in our own woods," and the envoi, in the revised wording of the Storisende edition, reads:

61

Seignior, although the severing daylight endures for a long while, I must be brave and worthy of Perion's love—nay, rather, of the love he gave me once. I may not grieve so long as no sort of evil troubles us in our own woods.

And on page 157, Demetrios is the speaker, the form of the passage is the same as that above and the refrain consists of variations of the expression, "I entreat of every person—only compassion and pardon."

The final contrapuntal experiment in this book is found on page 182 and is, according to Mr. Cabell, rather a faithful paraphrase of a poem by Giraud de Borneil. It reads:

Thou King of glory, veritable light, all-powerful deity! be pleased to succour faithfully my fair, sweet friend. The night that severed us has been long and bitter, the darkness has been shaken by bleak winds, but now the dawn is near at hand.

My fair sweet friend, be of good heart! We have been tormented long enough by evil dreams. Be of good heart, for the dawn is approaching! The east is astir. I have seen the orient star which heralds day. I discern it clearly, for now the dawn is near at hand.

My fair sweet friend, it is I, your servitor, who cry to you, *Be of good heart!* Regard the sky and the stars now growing dim, and you will see that I have been an untiring sentinel. It will presently fare the worse for those who do not recognize that the dawn is near at hand.

My fair sweet friend, since you were taken from me I have not ever been of a divided mind. I have kept faith, I have not failed you. Hourly I have entreated God and the Son of Mary to have compassion upon our evil dreams. And now the dawn is near at hand.

In *Chivalry* there is to be found only one passage, other than that already quoted, which seems contrapuntal in form. The plan is somewhat irregular, but frequent repetition of certain sounds is to be noticed in two paragraphs found on page 119 which are somewhat altered in the Storisende edition (page 127) and read as follows:

I am I! and I will so to live that I may face without shame not only God, but also my own scrutiny.

I love you: all my life long I am condemned to love you, Ysabeau, no matter what I may prefer: and you, too, dear Rosamund, I love, with a great difference. And I desire the power that you would give me, Ysabeau, and I desire the good which I would do with that power in the England which I or Blustering Roger Mortimer must rule, through edicts issued from your bedchamber: and I desire also to be the man that I would be if I were able now to choose death without any debate.

The next paragraph (in the revised passage) concludes, "he chooses his death without any debate," and the third paragraph ends: "I steadfastly protest that I am not very much afraid, and I choose death without any more debate."

CHAPTER VII

Something About Jurgen

JURGEN, as the most widely read of the books in the Biography, furnishes a particularly fine basis for a study of the prose counterpoint as it developed in Mr. Cabell's mind, the more so since this book was published just before *Figures of Earth*, and this latter volume is the one in which the contrapuntal form seems most frequently used in a clearly discernible verbal form.

Turning over the pages of *Jurgen*, the first paragraph to impress the reader seeking this planned prose is likely to be that on page 20 which reads:

"For in this garden," said the Centaur, "each man that ever lived has sojourned for a little while, with no company save his illusions. I must tell you again that in this garden are encountered none but imaginary creatures. And stalwart persons take their hour of recreation here, and go hence unaccompanied, to become aldermen and respected merchants and bishops, and to be admired as captains upon prancing horses, or even as kings upon tall thrones; each in his station thinking not at all of the garden ever any more. But now and then come timid persons, Jurgen, who fear to leave this garden without an escort: so these must need go hence with one or another imaginary creature, to guide them about alleys and bypaths, because imaginary creatures find little nourishment in the public highways and shun them. Thus must these timid persons skulk about obscurely with their diffident and skittish guides, and they do not ever venture willingly into the thronged places where men get horses and build thrones."

This is no more than a borderline passage but it has a poetic beauty and a rhythm and such recurring phrases as "in this garden," "imaginary creatures," "timid persons," "horses" and "thrones," give a hint of rhyme.

Then, coming to page 32, a distinct advance toward the full contrapuntal development is seen where Jurgen addresses Dorothy in three paragraphs having the same concluding sentence. And Mr. Cabell's informal definition of prose counterpoint is foreshadowed when Dorothy says to Jurgen at conclusion of his speech, "Why, this is excellent hearing, because I see you are converting your sorrow into the raw stuff of verses." It is interesting also to notice the corresponding placement of the words "answered" and "answer" in the first paragraph; "love" and "lovely" in the second, and "lived" and "life" in the third:

"Well, I am answered," said the pawnbroker: "and yet I know that this is not the final answer. Dearer than any hope of heaven was that moment when awed surmises first awoke as to the new strange loveliness which I had seen in the face of Dorothy. It was then I noted the new faint flush suffusing her face from chin to brow so often as my eyes encountered and found new lights in the shining eyes which were no longer entirely frank in meeting mine. Well, let that be, for I do not love Heitman Michael's wife.

"It is a grief to remember how we followed love, and found his service lovely. It is bitter to recall the sweetness of those vows which proclaimed her mine eternally,—vows that were broken in their making by prolonged and unforgotten kisses. We used to laugh at Heitman Michael then; we used to laugh at everything. Thus for a while, for a whole summer, we were as brave and comely and clean a pair of sweethearts as the world has known. But let that be, for I do not love Heitman Michael's wife.

"Our love was fair but short lived. There is none that may revive him since the small feet of Dorothy trod out this small love's life. Yet when this life of ours too is over—this parsimonious life which can allow us no more love for anybody,—must we not win back, somehow to that faith we vowed against eternity? and be content again in some fair colored realm? Assuredly I think this thing will happen. Well, but let that be, for I do not love Heitman Michael's wife."

Further development of the planned writing to the point where it may be re-arranged into something approximating verse-form is seen in the next passage, beginning on page 61. This passage is revised somewhat as to wording in the Storisende edition (where it appears on page 56) and this is the version here quoted, re-arranged into verses. It will be noticed that, apparently as a hint to the reader as to the proper arrangement, the last seven lines of the third verse are made separate quotations and so stand in the book in separate paragraphs, and themselves suggest the lines of a poem. Throughout, the witches of Amneram are the speakers and only the quotations (which compose the poem proper) are given here:

"*Note now, sweethearts, how high we pass*
over the wind-vexed heath,
where the dangling dead men creak and groan
in the gallows' iron chains.
Now the storm breaks loose as a hawk from the fowler,
and grave Queen Holda draws her tresses
over the moon's bright shield.
Now the bed is made, and the water drawn,
and we the bride's maids seek for the lass
who will be bride to Sclaug."

"Seek high, seek low, that quested maid!
Search for a strong-loined lass,
for to comfort a king who is old as love
and has outlived many brides!
Even now our grinning, dusty master
wakes from sleep, and his webbed, long fingers
shake to think of her flower-soft lips
who comes tonight to his lank embrace
and warms the ribs that our eyes have seen.
Who will be bride to Sclaug?"

"Note, too, note well, this wedding's gear,
all that a-questing ride!
That lass shall fare hence, on Phorgemon's saddle
in Cleopatra's shroud.
Then Will o' the Wisp shall marry this couple—"

"No, no! let Brachyotus!"
"No, be it Kitt with the candle-stick!"
"Eman hetan, a fight, a fight!"
"Oho, Tom Tumbler, 'ware of Stadlin!"
"Hast thou the marmaritin, Tib?"
"A ab hur hus!"
"Come, Bembo, come away!"

On page 64 is found another passage, compressed into a single paragraph but preserving the form ordinarily found in a succession of three paragraphs. The passage, with Jurgen as speaker, begins, "Hail to you, ladies, and farewell! for you and I have done with love." And it may be divided into three equal parts, each ending with the phrase "the end of all is death."

Frequent use of the word "love" in this passage also prepares the way for an experiment found on page 97 which is mentioned as part of a "Sirvente" Jurgen is making in praise of Guenevere, whom he addresses under another name.

These two paragraphs may be divided into fourteen lines, in groups of eight and six lines each with every line ending in the word love, if one disregards phrases that are not quoted and which here are given in parentheses to separate them from the poem proper:

"Lo, for I pray to thee, resistless love," (he descanted)
"that thou to-day make cry unto my love,
  to Phyllida whom I, poor Logreus, love
  so tenderly, not to deny me love!
  Asked why, say thou my drink and food is love,
  in days wherein I think and brood on love,
  and truly find naught good in aught save love,
  since Phyllida hath taught me how to love."

(Here Jurgen groaned with nicely modulated ardor; and he continued:)

"If she avow such constant hate of love
  as would ignore my great and constant love,
  plead thou no more! With listless lore of love
  woo Death resistlessly, resistless love,
  in place of her that hath such scorn of love
  as lends to Death the lure and grace I love."

One more passage, less definite in form, except for the repeated opening phrase, but possessing such rhythm and harmony in word sounds as to seem to merit quotation is found on page 303 of *Jurgen* and reads:

God of my grandmother, I cannot quite believe in You, and Your doings as they are recorded I find incoherent and a little droll. But I am glad the affair has been so arranged that You may always now be real to brave and gentle persons who have believed in and have worshipped and have loved You. To have disappointed them would have been unfair: and it is right that before the faith they had in You not even Koschei who made things as they are was able to be reasonable.

68

God of my grandmother, I cannot quite believe in You; but remembering the sum of love and faith that has been given You, I tremble. I think of the dear people whose living was confident and glad because of their faith in You: I think of them and in my heart contends a blind contrition, and a yearning, and an enviousness, and yet a tender sort of amusement colors all. Oh, God, there was never any other deity who had such dear worshippers as You have had, and You should be very proud of them.

God of my grandmother, I cannot quite believe in You, yet I am not as those who would come peering at You reasonably. I, Jurgen, see You only through a mist of tears. For You were loved by those whom I loved greatly very long ago: and when I look at You it is Your worshippers and the dear believers of old that I remember. And it seems to me that dates and manuscripts and the opinions of learned persons are very trifling things beside what I remember, and what I envy!

At three more places in this book one may find passages with contrapuntal characteristics but they probably should be regarded as one, or at most two, experiments because they are inter-related.

On page 338 Guenevere begins by saying to Jurgen: "Farewell to you, then Jurgen, for it is I that am leaving you forever."

At about the middle of this paragraph recurs the expression, "And it is I that am leaving you forever," and the paragraph ends with the same phrase.

Jurgen replies, "I could not see all this in you, not quite all this because of a shadow that followed me." And he concludes, "And so, farewell to you, Queen Guenevere, for it is a sorrowful thing and a very unfair thing that is happening."

Then, on page 343 Anaitis begins: "Farewell to you, then Jurgen, for it is I that am leaving you forever," and she too repeats this expression half way through and at the end of her discourse. And again Jurgen replies: "I could not see all this in you, not quite all this because of a shadow that followed me," and his conclusion, except for the name used, is the same as that addressed to Guenevere.

The third passage, on page 347 is related to the two preceding ones yet has sufficient structure to stand by itself as a contrapuntal experiment. Queen Helen says nothing to Jurgen "because there was no need," but he addresses her in three paragraphs each beginning, "And so farewell to you, Queen Helen!" and he concludes the third paragraph, "So it is necessary that I now cry farewell to you, Queen Helen: for I have failed in the service of my vision, and I deny you utterly!"

CHAPTER VIII

The Completed Circuit

EXAMPLES of the prose counterpoint are scarce in the next three books of the Biography. *The Line of Love* has hardly any passages that do much more than touch the borderline of the form, perhaps the closest approach being on page 180 in the passage beginning, "Lady Adeliza was a fair beauty." The following description is in two sections, each ending with the word "beauty" and in the Storisende edition, this is expanded by inclusion of a third part ending in the same word. Then follow two brief sections of descriptive matter (all of these in the same paragraph) each beginning with the word "proud."

The High Place has one approach to the form on page 43 in a passage beginning: "Then they spoke foolishly (replied Florian) because they spoke with pitiable inadequacy." He then praises Melior, ending the paragraph, "but presently I yawn and say they are not as Melior."

The next paragraph opens, "Her beauty is that beauty which women had in the world's youth, and whose components the old world forgets in this gray age." Wonderfully poetic references to Helen, Cleopatra, Semiramis, Erigone and Guenevere follow and the par-

71

agraph ends: "Therefore I cry again, I cry the name of Melior: and though none answers, I know that I cry upon the unflawed and living beauty which my own eyes have seen."

And the third paragraph completes the circuit with the ending: "I remember Melior, and I must rid myself of the fond foolish creature who is not as Melior."

A single passage in *Gallantry* seems worthy of quotation and this is reminiscent of the experiments found in *Domnei*. Beginning on page 146 one reads:

How did you know, Jack? How did you know that—things, invisible gracious things, went about the spring woods? . . . They are probably the heathen fauns and satyrs and such,—one feels somehow that they are all men. Don't you Jack? Well, when the elder gods were sent packing from Olympus there was naturally no employment left for these sylvan folk. So April took them into her service. Each year she sends them about every forest on her errands: she sends them to make the daffodil cups, for instance, which I suppose is difficult, for evidently they make them of sunshine; or to pencil the eyelids of the narcissi—narcissi are brazen creatures, Jack, and use a deal of kohl; or to marshal the fleecy young clouds about the sky; or to whistle the birds up from the south. Oh, she keeps them busy, does April! And 'tis true that if you be quite still you can hear them tripping among the dead leaves; and they watch you—with very bright, twinkling little eyes, I think,—but you never see them. And always, always there is that enormous whispering,—half-friendly, half-menacing,—as if the woods were trying to tell you something. 'Tis not only the foliage rustling. . . . No, I have often thought it sounded like some gigantic foreigner—some Titan probably,—trying in his own queer and outlandish language to tell you something very important, something that means a deal to you, and to you in particular. Has anybody ever understood him?

Turning again to page 92 of *From the Hidden Way* and "The Dotard Conjurer," which was mentioned

72

before in another connection, a further parallelism is noticed. In the third verse of this poem one reads:

> *And fear and beauty keep their heritage*
> *And breathe of something hidden in the woods*
> *Save birds, and trees, and flowers, and ravenous gnats,—*
> *For they are haunted by those messengers*
> *That April sends about our woods no more*
> *On primal errands. But in Avalon,*
> *Fern-carpeted untroubled Avalon,*
> *When April wakes and rises, with wind-blown hair*
> *And steadfast eyes—when at the tip of the world*
> *The sun takes heart a little,—then sturdy April*
> *Exults, and summons tricksy ministers*
> *To color and flaunt in low, yet-dreaming fields*
> *The first flush of the apple-blossoms; and marshal*
> *The stout spears of the daffodils; and guide*
> *Frail baby clouds about the lonely heavens;*
> *And polish frost-nipped stars; and re-awaken*
> *Warm gracious land-winds where the restive waters*
> *Shout to the glistening sands and hunger all night*
> *With impotent desire of the naked moon.*

Coming, then, to *Something About Eve* the reader again finds frequent passages having characteristics of the prose counterpoint. These vary in the definiteness of their verbal planning, but there are ten places in the book where, in Mr. Cabell's judgment, the term "contrapuntal prose" might with some justification be applied.

One notices, for example, on page 73 the apparent rhythm and the harmony of sound induced by repetition of the words "O Butterfly" and "repent" in the following paragraph:

"O Butterfly, O Gleaming One, your breakfast this day is disappointment, your fork is agony, and your napkin death. O

73

Butterfly, repent truly, abandon falsehood, put away deceit and flattery, cease thinking about your deluded lovers even remorsefully. Repent in verity, do not repent like the wildcat which repents with the fowl in its mouth without putting the fowl down. Where now is the artfulness which was yours, where are the high-hearted tricked lovers?—To-day all lies in the tomb. This world, O Butterfly, is a market-place: everyone comes and goes, both stranger and citizen. The last of your lovers is a pious friend, he assists the decreed course of this world."

And the whole twelfth chapter, beginning on page 86 may be regarded as written in prose counterpoint.

Gerald, looking into the mirror of Caer Omn, is drawn forward and has the experiences of several historical characters, or personages known to mythology, beginning with Prometheus. Near the beginning of the first long paragraph is the statement that he had preserved men and women from destruction "by the harshness and injustice of Heaven," and the paragraph ends with the phrase "Heaven's injustice." The next paragraph ends with the word "Heaven," and the following one concludes with a reference to "Heaven's will to destroy." The next paragraph, in which Gerald has the experiences of Judas, concludes, "he sang toward Heaven about his infamy"; near the end of the next paragraph he "reviled the will of Heaven"; the following paragraph concludes with a reference to "the ever-present malignity of Heaven"; the next ends, "Heaven pursued all men whom Heaven had not yet destroyed, ruthlessly," and in the remaining three paragraphs are other similar references until at the end, Gerald steps backward (completing the familiar circuit) and is released from the mirror's magic.

But, to notice, as has been done, only the recurrence

74

of a certain expression or word, variously handled, is to miss much that gives the passage its contrapuntal form. The chapter just mentioned is one of the places where the counterpoint can be seen by the discerning reader, but is not quite definite enough to be explained in terms of word usage. The plan lies more in the idea and general effect than in any verbal plan that might be pointed out.

On page 120 is found more than a paraphrasing (since it is an exact repetition) of a poem found in *From the Hidden Way*. The passage reads:

Said Tenjo: "I enter, proud and erect. I take my fill of delight imperiously, irrationally, and none punishes."

The priestess replied, "Not yet."

Tenjo said then, "But in three months, and in three months, and in three more months, the avenger comes forth, and mocks me by being as I am, and by being foredoomed to do as I have done, inevitably."

And on page 210 of *From the Hidden Way* under the title "The Cavern of Phigalia" appears all the quoted part of the above passage with addition only of the word "visibly" after "as I am" in the last sentence.

On page 143 of *Something About Eve* is a conversation between Gerald and his son that has some contrapuntal characteristics, although the verbal proof is rather indefinite and, on page 225 begins a chapter dealing with the six words of wisdom known to Solomon which also is carefully balanced and planned. The discourse of Merlin, beginning on page 229 also might be regarded as contrapuntal and the form becomes less doubtful on page 265 when Gerald speaks in three paragraphs each ending in the phrase "useful to ro-

75

mantic art." The discourse of the Bishop, beginning on page 286, is similar in form, each paragraph ending, "and it was all very discouraging."

Somewhat more complex in form is the passage beginning on page 319. "What is it men desire?" asks the woman. The Adversary says that men do not know what they desire and concludes, "Yes, it is well that Antan has perished."

In the next two paragraphs the woman speaks, ending each time, "But men want more," and in a third paragraph she concludes, "Yes, it is very well that Antan has perished." The Adversary speaks again and when the woman replies she concludes, "At last, Antan has fallen: it is very well." The Adversary then concludes, "But Antan has fallen: and after that foolishness at least my people will not be following any more."

The final passage in this book to be noticed is that beginning on page 323. Gerald is the speaker in five paragraphs, all of which are given an harmonic effect by verbal repetitions such as are illustrated by the following brief quotation of the first paragraph:

I have come out of my native home on a gainless journeying with no profit in it; yet there has been pleasure in that journeying. I do not complain. Let every man that must journey, without ever knowing why, from the dark womb of his mother to the dark womb of his grave, take pattern by me!

And the connection between these paragraphs is illustrated by the similarity in the sound of the conclusion of the first and of the second which ends:

I did not ride the divine steed to my journey's end: but a part of the way I rode quite royally.

Passing on to *The Certain Hour*, the reader is likely

to find in this volume only one passage of prose counterpoint. This, beginning on page 38, is a paraphrase of the poem "One End of Love" to be found on page 37 of *From the Hidden Way* and both should be read in their entirety if the parellelism is to be studied, but brief quotations will indicate its nature.

The prose passage opens:

Biatritz said, "It is a long while since we two met."
He that had been her lover all his life said, "Yes."

She was no longer the most beautiful of women, no longer his be-hymned Belhs Cavaliers—you may read elsewhere how he came to call her that in all his canzons—but only a fine and gracious stranger. It was uniformly gray, that soft plentiful hair, where once such gold had flamed as dizzied him to think of even now; there was no crimson in those thinner lips; and candor would have found her eyes less wonderful than those Raimbaut has dreamed of very often among an alien and a hostile people.

The poem begins:

It is long since we met,—she said.
I answered,—Yes.

She is not fair,
But very old now, and no gold
Gleams in that scant gray withered hair
Where once much gold was: and, I think,
Not easily might one bring tears
Into her eyes, which have become
Like dusty glass.

The prose passage ends:

Thus the evening passed, and at its end Makrisi followed the troubadour to his regranted fief of Vaquieras. This was a chill and brilliant night, swayed by a frozen moon so powerful that no stars showed in the unclouded heavens, and everywhere the bogs were curdled with thin ice. An obdurate wind swept like a knife-blade across a world which even in its spring seemed very old.

And the last verse of the poem reads:

And we ride homeward now, and I
Ride moodily: my palfrey jogs
Along a rock-strewn way the moon
Lights up for us; yonder the bogs
Are curdled with thin ice; the trees
Are naked; from the barren wold
The wind comes like a blade aslant
Across a world grown very old.

The Cream of the Jest contains three passages contrapuntal in nature and the first of these, beginning on page 11, is a single paragraph in which "beauty" is the thematic word, as is shown by the following quotation:

Assuredly, it was you of whom blind Homer dreamed, comforting endless night with visions of your beauty, as you sat in a bright fragrant vaulted chamber weaving at a mighty loom, and embroidering on tapestry the battles men were waging about Troy because of your beauty; and very certainly it was to you that Hermes came over fields of violets and parsley, where you sang magic rhymes sheltered by an island cavern, in which cedar and citronwood were burning—and, calling you Calypso, bade you release Odysseus from the spell of your beauty. Sophocles, too, saw you bearing an ewer of bronze, and treading gingerly among gashed lamentable corpses, lest your beloved dead be dishonored: and Sophocles called you Antigone, praising your valor and your beauty. And when men named you Bombyca, Theocritus also sang of your grave drowsy voice and your feet carven of ivory, and of your tender heart and all your honey-pale sweet beauty.

Then, on page 14, Horvendile speaks in four paragraphs. The first of these may rather easily be made to fall into hexameters:

When I behold the skylark move in perfect joy
toward its love the sun, and, growing drunk with joy,

78

forget the use of wings, so that it topples from
the height of heaven, I envy the bird's fate. I, too,
would taste that ruinous mad moment of communion,
there in heaven, and my heart dissolves in longing.

The next two paragraphs of this speech do not scan so easily, but the poetic spirit remains: and this is not surprising since, Mr. Cabell confesses, the passage is rather faithfully paraphrased from a poem by Bernard de Ventadour.

Ailas! how little do I know of love!—I, who was once deluded by the conceit that I was all wise in love. For I am unable to put aside desire for a woman whom I must always love in vain. She has bereft me of hope, and all joy in the world, and she has left me nothing save dreams and regrets.

Never have I been able to recover my full senses since that moment when she first permitted me to see myself mirrored in her bright eyes. Hey, fatal mirrors! which flattered me too much! for I have sighed ever since I beheld my image in you. I have lost myself in you, like Narcissus in his fountain.

The final paragraph adapts itself to the following, slightly irregular, verse form:

Since nothing will avail to move my lady—
not prayers nor righteous claims or mercy—
and she desires my homage now no longer,
I shall have nothing more to say of love.
I must renounce love, and abjure it utterly.
I must regard her whom I love
as one no longer living. I must, in fine,
do that which I prepare to do;
and afterward I must depart into eternal exile.

The third passage in this book, beginning on page 209, includes six paragraphs. The first reads:

I am sad tonight, for I remember that I once loved a woman. She was white as the moon; her hair was a gold cloud; she had

79

untroubled eyes. She was so fair that I longed for her until my heart was as the heart of a God. But she sickened and died: worms had their will of her, not I. So I took other women, and my bed was never lonely. Bright poisonous women were brought to me from beyond the sunset, from the Fortunate Islands, from Invallis and Planasia even; and these showed me nameless endearments and many curious perverse pleasures. But I was not able to forget that woman who was denied me because death had taken her: and I grew a-weary of love, for I perceived that all which has known life must suffer death.

Four paragraphs of about the same length, which follow this one, each end, "all which has known life must suffer death," and then comes this shorter "envoi":

For death is mighty, and against it naught can avail: it is terrible and strong and cruel, and a lover of bitter jests. And presently, whatever I have done or studied or dreamed, I must lie helpless where worms will have their will of me, and neither the worms nor I will think it odd, because we have both learned— by how countless attestings!—that all which has known life must suffer death.

And this concluding passage in the last book of the Biography proper, not only completes a circuit in itself, but it harks back to *Figures of Earth* and the passage beginning, "What price would be sufficient to re-purchase the rich spoils of death?" Thus a larger circuit is symbolized once again in verbal form.

The epilogue to the Biography, *Straws and Prayer-Books*, contains two passages which might also be classed as contrapuntal. On page 15 the author begins, "And somehow, now that, comfortably replete with luncheon, I approach my epilogue, now it is in my mind to make verses rather than to discourse in sober and reasonable prose."

He looks through a window and sees "The world, in preparing to be very beautiful, is for the while disheveled looking: and it suggests to me, without any stepping stones of exact analogy, a handsome woman, defamatorily clad in a shabby green dressing-gown poised before her mirror, with her hair already partially loosened in order that she may prepare for a festival."

"It is a fine festival for which the world makes ready," the next paragraph begins; and the following paragraph concludes, "and it is in my mind to make verses."

There is another paragraph, dealing with memories, and then one beginning, "Now it is in my mind to make verses about this festival, but I lack any matter, here again that plainly prompts to versifying. We older persons must sit out . . . we dare at most to attend as chaperons. . . ."

Explaining, in the next paragraph, that older people have other things to do, he concludes, "I merely note that we are but, at best, the chaperons at this festival for which the April world is preparing. So we must look on benevolently, and must preserve decorum, and also must not ever concede what urge it is that prompts this festival. . . . still, it is in my mind to make verses. . . ."

The final passage of counterpoint, quite appropriately, contains a statement of the "creed" of the novelist, containing those general tenets which he will, at most, admit to himself, very secretly. This statement begins on page 42.

"Imprimis," he begins, "I play, when all is said, with common sense and piety, as my fellows appraise these matters, and with death also." This paragraph concludes: "And my rational standards can be adhered to, I consider, with more safety if they are kept concealed."

The five following paragraphs, starting "Item" all conclude with statements as to the necessity or desirability of concealment. They deal, severally, with his real beliefs, which are worthwhile only as playthings; his ideas, which he is unable to say will not be changed completely by tomorrow; lack of concern with human life as a whole; the resistless hunger to escape from use and wont, and the determination not to plagiarize from nature or real life.

The final paragraph, following this series, reads:

Item, let us avoid, also, the narcotizing perils of reverence. And let us, above all, avoid disastrous candors, and say boldly none of these things. Let us who "write" protest that we have no concealments, that we expose ourselves entire, and that our unselfish aim is to benefit and entertain other persons, the while that we play ceaselessly with common-sense and piety and death.

82

CHAPTER IX

Sundry Devices of the Economist

AT outset of this paper it was suggested that the methods of Mr. Cabell, when he "plays" at being the creator of a universe, are economical, material being carefully considered and adapted to his uses and a verbal gem, cast aside once as unimportant, being retrieved at times to flash brilliantly in a newly devised setting. His use of the same material for prose and verse passages in some instances has been noticed.

Further to illustrate this argument it is necessary to refer to a tale they tell in Richmond-in-Virginia which has to do with *The Reviewer*—a fortnightly, later a monthly, magazine which began to be published there in the year 1920. Starting as the "play-thing" of a little group of literary enthusiasts, this magazine quickly attained some degree of national prominence, particularly because of the distinguished names appearing in its list of contributors despite the bland statement of the editors that "payment for such MSS. as may be found available will be in fame, not specie." This much is fact.

But the tale is that one contributor to *The Reviewer* undertook to criticise the editors for their lack of economy, pointing especially to their wasteful habit of leaving parts of pages without printing matter on them, thus wasting valuable white paper and he waved aside their argument that filler of proper length was not always available.

In the outcome, as some, but not all they in Richmond, aver, it was agreed that Mr. Cabell should inculcate this principle of economy by means of a concrete example while the editors, for their part, should deal fairly with him by shedding no light on this arrangement so that the shadow of suspicion might not fall upon him. So far runs the tale. Now, as to other recorded facts:

In October 1921 was issued the first number of the second volume of *The Reviewer*, and all its pages neatly were filled with printed matter. On page 9, for example, a contribution by Julia M. Peterkin was concluded at some little distance from the bottom of the page, yet the remaining space was not sufficient to accommodate a poem by George Stirling which, accordingly, was started at the top of page 10.

But the space which might otherwise have been wasted was filled in the following manner:

DICTATED BUT NOT READ
by Burwell Washington

Do not be vexed unduly if you find no meaning in this paragraph. For this paragraph was placed here simply because here happened to be a vacancy that needed filling. The foolish, therefore, will find in it foolishness, and will say "Bother!" The wise, as wisdom goes, will reflect that the paragraph was placed here without its consent being asked; that no wit nor large significance was loaned it by its creator; and that it will be forgotten with the turning of the one page wherein it figures unimportantly. So do you turn the page forthwith, in just the carefree fashion of old nodding Time as he skims over the long book of life: and do you say either "Bother!" or "Brother!" as your wits prompt.

Thus was the page very neatly filled, leaving space for not a single line more.

And, on page 11 of the same issue was another and slightly larger space that needed filling, which need was satisfied by the following:

PREHISTORICS
by Henry Lee Jefferson

A traveller came anciently to a walled city. "And I had often heard of your city," he said, when he had inspected the place, "but the half of its wonders had not been told to me."

They answered him, modestly, as was the manner of those far-off days: "Indeed, we cannot deny that our city was the cradle of all this nation, nor that it was the begetter of all civil and religious liberty, of statesmanship and patriotism and every virtue, nor that it is the only stronghold in these degenerate days, of all true culture and morality. Our men are the bravest and most chivalrous that have ever lived, our women the most beautiful and chaste. No other place has a history so glorious as has our city, no other place may be compared with us to-day in prosperity and virtue, and never at any time in the future shall any other city equal the least of our glories."

"All this is true," replied the traveller, "and for all these things, and for other excellences too, do I unfeignedly honor you and your city, but—"

Whereupon in apprehension lest that "But" prove the beginning of a hint as to their city's having some fault, they abolished the traveller with paving-stones, after the manner of those far-off days.

And here again the writing ends at just the proper place to give to the page a nicely balanced appearance.

85

In all the years since this issue of *The Reviewer* was printed, readers have looked in vain for other writings under the names of Burwell Washington and Henry Lee Jefferson. Indeed, so far as can be ascertained, the only other printed reference to either of them is to be found on page 103 of the November 1921 issue of this same magazine. Here the department "Things in General," ordinarily rather lengthy, is found filling (once again, very neatly) less than half a page.

It begins:

We always enjoy hearing from our contributors. Mr. Henry Lee Jefferson, for example, demands to know how we dared change the title of his Our City Too to Prehistorics. The answer is that we have lived in Richmond for some time, and plan to continue living there. . . . Mr. James Branch Cabell wants to be told why we said Lord Tiverton was "attained" when he was, actually, attainted. We refer him to the printers. . . . Mr. Burwell Washington also complains about the title of his article, lamenting that "but" was spelt with a large B. We don't care. . . .

To queries of the curious neither the nominal editors of the magazine nor Mr. Cabell would admit knowledge of the identity of Mr. Washington and Mr. Jefferson and it seemed that their work had been forgotten "with the turning of a page."

But when, in September 1927, there was issued Mr. Cabell's *Something About Eve*, some readers noticed, beginning on page 164 of the first kalki edition of the book, a chapter headed "The Paragraph of the Sphinx." And in this they read that Gerald Musgrave, in his journeying toward "Antan, the land of the third truth," arrived at the outskirts of Turoine and there came upon a Sphinx "who lay there writing with a black pen in a large black-covered book like a ledger."

After some preliminary conversation Gerald inquired as to what the Sphinx might be writing and she replied: "You find me just now in some difficulty with my book. You conceive that there has to be an opening paragraph. It would not be possible to leave out the first paragraph . . . and this paragraph ought to sum up all things, so to speak . . . and it is with this paragraph that I am just now having trouble."

Gerald admitted that he was somewhat a connoisseur of the art of letters and suggested that, if the Sphinx would read him what she had written, he might be able to straighten out her difficulty.

The following dialogue then is recorded:

"Do not be vexed unduly," the Sphinx then said, "if you can find no meaning in this paragraph—"

"I shall not be excessively censorious, I assure you. No beginner is expected to excel in any art."

"For this paragraph was placed here simply because there happened to be a vacancy which needed filling—"

"I quite understand that. So let us get on!"

But there was no hurrying the diffident Sphinx. "The foolish, therefore," the Sphinx continued in shy explanation, "will find in it foolishness, and will say 'Bother!' The wise, as wisdom goes, will reflect that this paragraph was placed here without its consent being asked; that no wit nor large significance was loaned it by its creator; and that it will be forgotten with the turning of the one page wherein it figures unimportantly—"

"No doubt it will be!" said Gerald, now speaking a little impatiently, "but let us get on to this famous paragraph!"

"—So do you turn the page forthwith, in just the care-free fashion of old nodding Time as he skims over the long book of life: and do you say 'Bother!' or 'Brother!' as your wits prompt."

"I will, I assure you, the moment your book is published. But why do you keep talking about your paragraph? why do you not read me what you have written?"

"I have just done so," replied the Sphinx. "I have not been talking. I have been reading ever since I said, 'Do you not be vexed' and now I have read you the whole paragraph."

Gerald said, "Oh!" He scratched his long chin a bit blankly. He approached the monster, and leaning over one forepaw, he read for himself in that black ledger the paragraph of the Sphinx.

Then Gerald said, "But what comes next?"

"Were I to answer that question you would be wiser than I. And of course nobody can ever be wiser than the Sphinx."

"But is that as far as you have written?"

"That is as far as anybody has written," said the Sphinx, "as yet."

"In all these centuries you have not got beyond that one paragraph?"

"Now, do you not see my difficulty? I needed an opening paragraph which would sum up all things, so to speak, and all the human living which men keep pestering me to explain. And when I had written it there was not anything left over to put in the second paragraph."

In the subsequent conversation as to the possibility of there being any second paragraph, the Sphinx, although often interrupted, repeats once again this paragraph and, under the author's creative touch, the reader is made to see more clearly that in this bit of filler material is summed up an entire attitude toward life: the conception of life from an individual standpoint as a brief bit in the long book of Life; a bit which may to some persons seem meaningless; the idea that the individual is placed here without his consent being asked and that, perhaps, no wit nor large significance was loaned to him by his creator, and that each one will be forgotten with the turning of one page in the long book in which he figures unimportantly.

Another, though less striking, example of the renewed use of a seemingly forgotten passage also was seen in November 1927 when there was issued the first illustrated edition of *The Cream of the Jest.*

By way of author's note Mr. Cabell, among other things, confesses to his inability to understand why the descendants of Manuel chose to settle in so out of the way a place as Lichfield and he continues:

John Charteris, though,—I now recall,—did once go a bit farther, and did refer me to the eleventh fable of his own *Foolish Prince.* That apologue I therefore in this place append, as the sole answer which I have ever been able to extort from these over-willful characters.

And the fable is called

PREHISTORICS

As was the manner of those far-off days, the traveller came mounted upon a hippogriffin to the bronze gates of a walled city. "And I had often heard of your city," he said, when he had inspected the place, "but not one-tenth of its wonders," he added, upon the excellent principle that there is nothing like the decimal system,—"had ever been told to me."

They answered him modestly, as was the manner of those far-off days: "Indeed, we cannot deny that our city was the cradle of this nation, nor that it was the first begetter of all civil and religious liberty, of statesmanship and patriotism and every virtue, nor that it is the only stronghold, in these degenerate times, of exalted culture and morality. We cannot deny our men are the bravest and most chivalrous that ever loved, our women the most beautiful and chaste. Nay, more than this! because of our exceeding great love for candor, we cannot even deny that no other place shows in the past a history so soul-inspiring as does our city; that to-day there is no other place may be compared with us in prosperity nor in contentment nor in our wholesome way of living; and that never at any time in the future shall any other city equal the least of our glories."

"Now I also, no word of this do I deny," replied the traveller,

89

with such frank enthusiasm as was the manner of those far-off days. "For many excellencies do I unfeignedly admire you and your city. Yet—"

Whereafter, very promptly, lest that "yet" should prove the beginning of a hint as to their city's displaying some fault, they abolished the traveller and his hippogriffin also, with paving stones, as was the manner of those far-off days.

At least a co-incidence is to be noticed in the fact that this is quoted as from the *eleventh* fable of the *Foolish Prince* and the article by the much-be-plagiarized Henry Lee Jefferson was printed on the *eleventh* page of that issue of *The Reviewer* in which it appeared.

And so, omitting any daring forecast as to what may appear in one of Mr. Cabell's books at some time in the future, and certainly without any guess as to the identity of the author, but with, perhaps, a broad wink to the discerning, it seems permissible here to quote also from page 86 of the November 1921 issue of *The Reviewer:*

COBWEBS AND IRON
by Claiborne Hauks Anderson

Then one returned,—in gold and violet,
Clad utterly, even as those Viewers that were
The bane of Orn's old murderers—crying, "Sir,
*   Albeit Love's last euphrasy beset*
*   Tomorrow's dawn, this day abides to wet*
Love's lids with weeping; whose lithe harp-player,
With fluent fingers resonant of her
*   Thou knowest of, seeks mirth, no less. And yet*
What bifold shadows quest life's baffled strain,
*   Horse-tongued and dominant!"*

*   "It is enough,"*
I answered, "that this multiversant Love

Seeks dawn, and always dawn's light loss of gain."
— Then ended, leaving others to explain
  The meaning of the dozen lines above.

CHAPTER X

Reflections
As to Mirrors and Pigeons

SOME years ago the writer of this paper was so thoughtless as to ask Mr. Cabell to explain the secret of the mirror and the pigeons: "thoughtless" seems now the proper word to describe this action because reflection has made the situation then existing seem analogous to that confronting Gerald Musgrave when he declined to enter Antan.

"After dark," one reads in *Something About Eve*, "Antan always displayed eight lights, six of them grouped together in the middle of the vista with the general effect of a cross, and the other two showing much farther to the northwest. About these never-varying huge lights Gerald had formed at least twenty delightful theories, all plausible as long as you remained upon Mispec Moor, whereas if you went to Antan not more at most than one of these theories could be true.

"To go to Antan thus meant the destruction of no less than nineteen rather beautiful ideas as to those lights alone. . . . "

So, the writer thoughtlessly might have robbed himself of perhaps twenty delightful theories as to the significance of the mirror and pigeons—each theory based on a separate reference in the Biography—had not Mr. Cabell been discreet enough to reply: "There are reasons, which I consider now with real regret, why I cannot explain to you the secret of the mirror and the pigeons. I am however at liberty to say that the reference is by no means to a mere 'myth'."

But even realization of the advantage of not being confined to one theory regarding Mr. Cabell's favorite mystery has not served to quench the desire to understand these enigmatic references, and the result has been the working out of an hypothesis. This suggested explanation is given, however, with the understanding that it is not to prejudice the right of any person— including the author—to formulate and to believe in any other theory or theories that he may elect.

In the first place, then, it would seem after considering all the references to mirrors and pigeons in the Biography that these objects are devices used in some branch of sorcery.

Jurgen in his first encounter with Mother Sereda sees, hung above a table in her apartment, "a wicker cage containing a blue bird, and another wicker cage containing three white pigeons." After he has asked her to let him have one of her Wednesdays she offers him the blue bird, which he declines to accept. "So Mother Sereda took from the wall the wicker cage containing the three white pigeons: and going before him . . . she led the way into a courtyard, where, sure enough, they found tethered a he-goat. Of a dark blue color this beast was, and his eyes were wiser than the eyes of a beast. Then Jurgen set about that which Mother Sereda said was necessary."

And here it is to be recalled that the Sabbat, "a meeting attended by all witches in satisfactory diabolical standing" was graced also by the company of the devil who "usually attended in the form of a monstrous goat," according to the statement of Mr. Richard Harrowby, as recorded in *The Cream of the Jest*.

Returning to *Jurgen* we read, "In his hand Merlin held a small mirror, about three inches square, from which he raised his dark eyes puzzlingly.

"'I have been talking to my fellow ambassador, Dame Anaitis: and I have been wondering, Messire de Logreus, if you have ever reared white pigeons.'

"Jurgen looked at the little mirror. 'There was a woman of the Leshy not long ago showed me an employment to which one might put the blood of white pigeons. She too used a mirror. I saw what followed, but I must tell you candidly that I understood nothing of the ins and outs of the affair'."

From which it would seem that the use to which the sorcerer puts the mirror and pigeons is in establishing a communication with beings or a world that is supramundane.

Another example of the use of these devices in some form of sorcery is to be found in *Something About Eve* when "Horvendile gave Gerald a queer word of power, and Horvendile took out of his pocket a little mirror three inches square. You heard in the duskiness the flapping of small vigorous wings. Then three white pigeons stood among the swine, at the feet of Horvendile. He did what was requisite: and Gerald thus came straightway into a place that was not unfamiliar."

In this same book is found a more definite sugges-

94

tion as to the significance of mirrors and pigeons when the six words of power and wisdom known to Solomon are mentioned, among them "the word of the mirror. It was spoken, and before him stood a wicker cage containing three pigeons. Beside this cage lay a small mirror three inches square."

By applying the other five words to the things mentioned over which it is obvious that they were intended to give power, it appears in the elimination that the mirror and pigeons made him master of "the elemental spirits and the ghosts of the dead." And, as to the one word of power not known to Solomon, "his little mirror showed him that word, as it showed every other thing; but the word was written in a language which he could not read."

Also in this book is found the following conversation between Gerald and the Sylan:

"And this Queen Freydis has a mirror which must, they say, be faced by those persons who venture into the goal of all the gods of men—"

"That mirror too," said Gerald airily, "I may be needing. Mirrors are employed in many branches of magic."

And Glaum said: "For one, I would not meddle with that mirror. Even in the land of Dersam, where a mirror is sacred, we do not desire any dealings with the mirror of the Hidden Children and with those strange reflections which are unclouded by either good or evil."

Now, here is found no mention of the pigeons, nor is the size of the mirror specified and so, there seems no bar to the supposition that the small mirror used with the pigeons in sorcery may be a symbol representative of the "mirror of the Hidden Children."

To understand the significance of this last phrase it is necessary to refer to *Figures of Earth* and to a passage in which neither mirrors nor pigeons are mentioned, but which seems to furnish the only clue as to the nature of the mirror of Freydis.

Ruric, young clerk to Dom Manuel, has been tempted to go out through the third window of Ageus into the scented dusk that the count of Poictesme is dubious about entering in person; and, on his return, Ruric replies to the questioning of his master:

"Count Manuel, I will tell you a merry story of how a great while ago our common grandmother Eve was washing her children one day near Eden when God called to her. She hid away the children that she had not finished washing: and when the good God asked if all her children were there, with their meek little heads against His knees, to say their prayers to Him, she said Yes. So God told her that what she had tried to hide from God should be hidden from men: and He took away the unwashed children and made a place for them where everything stays young, and where there is neither good nor evil, because the children are unstained by human sin and unredeemed by Christ's dear blood."

And, in *Straws and Prayer-Books*, Mr. Cabell and Mr. Harrowby have the following conversation, Cabell speaking first:

"Men, it was whispered, had, for however brief a while, escaped from the obligations and restraints and, above all, from the tediousness of workaday life,— that tediousness which people have always tried to vary and color, under every sort of human civilization, with so many forms of fiction. . . ."

96

"But you have the ladder of the seven metals, and you know perfectly well the secret of the mirror and the pigeons—"

"That," I protested, "isn't the point!" . . . For I was in fact not at all concerned with the exact amount of truth upon which these legends were based. The point with me, was that man has since time's beginning wanted such tales to be true; and that these stories illustrated man's immemorial and universal desire to escape from the self-imposed routine of his daily life. Man had always believed that he could do this by the aid of wizardry: and in this belief, as I now saw, he had been always and perfectly right.

Here, then, are suggestions that there is a world wherein reside beings untouched by the ravages of time or sin and having nothing to do with questions of good or evil. And it is suggested that men may, through the aid of wizardry, come into contact with this world.

Consider now the statement of Evarvan of the Mirror, as made to Gerald in *Something About Eve:*

"There is for you through my mirror's aid an open way to contentment. You shall know an untruth, and that untruth will make you free: the doings of the world . . . will then run by you like a little stream of shallow bickering waters: and you will heed none of these things, but only that loveliness which all youth desires and no man ever finds save through the mirror's aid. You will live among bright shadows very futilely: yes: but you will be happy."

And this idea of the mirror as a means of entering the abode of the Hidden Children seems confirmed by another passage in the same book when Gerald, being

97

drawn into the mirror of Caer Omn, views "with lively admiration a throng of strange and lovely beings such as he had not known in Lichfield."

One may recall also the passages in *Figures of Earth* when Queen Freydis tells of her kingdom that lies "behind this veil of human sight and sense" and when Manuel says, "He that has willed to look upon Queen Freydis does not dread to consort with serpents nor with swine (there were swine present when Horvendile employed the mirror and pigeons) he faces the mirror wherein a man beholds himself without self-deceiving; he views the blood (of white pigeons?) that drips from his soiled hands, and knows that this, too, was needed."

Thus, the mirror and pigeons seem firmly linked with the familiar Cabellian doctrine of escape from reality. And the mirror is associated with the sigil that was to Kennaston, in *The Cream of the Jest*, a means of communication with that "bright shadow" whom he named Ettarre, for in this book we read:

"Ah, yes, those little magics, those futile troubling necromancies that are wrought by portraits and un-familiar rooms and *mirrors and all time-worn glittering objects*. . . . These are the little magics that have no large power, but how inconsequently do they fret upon men's heart-strings!"

Here it is seen that the mirror and such a time-worn glittering object as the sigil may be classed together in their effects.

Two passages in *The Cream of the Jest* are those which most often arouse curiosity as to the secret of the mirror and the pigeons. In the first of these the "personage" tells Kennaston "Those portions of your book relating to the sigil of Scoteia struck me as being too explicit. . . . Do you think it quite wise? I seem to recall a phrase about birds—"

As Kennaston looks at him, bewilderedly, the personage takes from his pocket "a small square mirror, which he half-exhibited, but retained secretively in the palm of his hand" and he says: "I am presupposing that, as a country-gentleman, you have raised white pigeons, Mr. Kennaston?"

When he is considering the incident later Kennaston wonders if the reference to mirrors and pigeons was some pass-word unknown to him and he reflects: "What could a little mirror, much less pigeons, have to do with this bit of metal?—except that this bit of metal (the sigil), too, reflected light so that the strain tired your eyes, thus steadily to look down upon the thing."

Thus, at the end of a suggestion that the sigil and the mirror are unrelated, their similarity is re-emphasized.

The second passage that attracts attention in this book has to do with the meeting of Kennaston and the prelate who asks if Kennaston has followed the example of his uncle in raising white pigeons, and "Kennaston saw that the prelate now held a small square mirror in his left hand."

The prelate says: "yet, in dealing with the sigil of Scoteia—or so it would seem to me—you touched upon subjects which had better be left undisturbed."

And again Kennaston feels that he is being tested, especially when the prelate admits that many men in public life carry such mirrors as his and even suggests that there may be some secret which they hold in common.

99

And these two suggestions as to the desirability of keeping from the general public the secret of the mirror and the pigeons is in accord with the sentiment expressed in the tale about Dr. Herrick entitled "Concerning Corinna" in *The Certain Hour*. Here are described dealings with a world beyond the veil of sight and sense and it is suggested that such experiences are not to be given to the public but are to be talked of only between the discerning elect.

In keeping with these suggestions as to secrecy is the attempt, near the end of *The Cream of the Jest* to discount the mystery of the mirror and the pigeons, when we read: "The coincidence of the mirrors was quaint, but in itself came to less than nothing; for as touches the two questions as to white pigeons, the proverb alluded to by the personage, concerning the bird that fouls its own nest, is fairly familiar, and the prelate's speech was the most natural of prosaic inquiries. What these two men had said and done, in fine, amounted to absolutely nothing until transfigured in the crucible of an ardent imagination by the curious literary notion that human life as people spend it is purposeful and clearly motivated."

But here is a restriction rather than a denial,—the incidents, it is admitted, *are* significant when transfigured in the crucible of an ardent imagination by the curious literary notion that human life is purposeful and clearly motivated.

In *The Silver Stallion* is another reference to pigeons, but this seems merely casual rather than significant, Guivric coming into a room in which "white pigeons were walking about and eating barley."

A new idea as to the characteristics of the mirror is suggested in this book however. When the suitors of Morvyth returned with the treasures they had won, "Prince Duneval of Ore said nothing. His mutely tendered offering was a small mirror about three inches square. Morvyth looked into this mirror: and what she saw in it was very little like a sumptuous dark young girl. She hastily put aside that gleaming and over-wise counselor: and the queen's face was troubled, because there was no need to ask what mirror Duneval had fetched to her from out of Antan."

And this new idea as to the characteristics of the mirror of the Hidden Children is supported, in one respect at least, by the passage in *Figures of Earth* in which Manuel, contesting with Freydis, finds himself grasping "a thick slab of crystal, like a mirror, wherein he could see himself quite clearly. Just as he really was, he who was not at all familiar with such mirrors, could see Count Manuel, housed in a little wet dirt with old inveterate stars adrift about him everywhither: and the spectacle was enough to frighten anybody."

Still other testimony as to the use of the mirror in revealing things as they actually are is found in the statement of Maya to Gerald in *Something About Eve:* "It is said that Queen Freydis holds her mirror up to nature, and that she does not scruple to hold this mirror up to her disreputable visitors too. . . . And there is no flaw in it, people say, no distortion of any kind, no flattering in it, and no kindly exaggeration."

And in *The Cream of the Jest* when Kennaston asks about the small square mirror which Cromwell and

101

other famous men also carried he is told: "Yes, that mirror aids them. In that mirror they can see only themselves. So the mirror aids them toward the ends they chose, with open eyes."

And in this last statement a suggestion is found as to how the idea of the mirror as revealing reality may be combined with the conception of the mirror and pigeons as means of access to the world of the Hidden Children.

So far we have been dealing with the significance and the purpose of the mirror and pigeons, rather than the manner in which they work. But, is it not plausible to suppose that human beings can establish communication with the world of the Hidden Children only by first looking into the unconsolingly frank mirror without a flaw? Those who are satisfied with what they see go on, as Cromwell and the personage and the prelate did, becoming successes in the material world. But others, having realized their deficiencies as human beings, are filled with such self-loathing that they must perforce seek more perfect beings and a more perfect world.

These unsatisfied persons journey, through the aid of the mirror and pigeons, toward Suskind's "April scented dusk," or Freydis' "Antan, the goal of all the Gods of men."

Still unanswered remains the question of how the mirror and pigeons operate other than by creating the desire for a glimpse of the abode of the Hidden Children.

To those easily satisfied it may be enough to suggest that a small mirror is an excellent device with which to look backward and "Antan" is rather easily translated "yesteryear." Certainly there is reason for concluding that only in memories of the past may perfection be found and Mr. Cabell himself seems, at times, to concur in this view.

But some there are doomed to an "eternally unsatisfied hungering in search of beauty," and these the writer would refer back to *The Cream of the Jest* where "he who wills may read", if he be aided by the sigil of Scoteia, one of the most frank confessions yet made by Mr. Cabell of his purposes and his ideas.

Lynchburg, Va.,
April 1928.

103

❧ *Fifteen hundred copies of this book have been printed for* RANDOM HOUSE *New York, on Rittenhouse Laid paper by Richard W. Ellis, The Georgian Press in the month of September,* 1928

No. 1499

CPSIA information can be obtained
at www.ICGtesting.com
Printed in the USA
BVHW012338080819
555425BV00022B/160/P

9 781162 608259